Coping with Separation and Divorce

Cassell Lifeguides

Cassell 'Lifeguides' are books for today's way of life. The increasing trend towards a 'self-help society' is an indication of the need for reliable, helpful information in book form, as less and less advice is offered elsewhere.

With this series, Cassell furthers its reputation as a publisher of useful, practical self-help books and tackles subjects which are very much in line with today's lifestyles and problems. As people become increasingly aware that situations need to be looked at from all sides, they can turn to these books for realistic advice and encouragement.

Coping with Separation and Divorce

Jean Stuart

CASSELL

Cassell Publishers Limited
Artillery House, Artillery Row
London SW1P 1RT

First published 1989

ISBN 0-304-31668-7

British Library Cataloguing in Publication Data

Stuart, Jean
   Coping with separation and divorce.
   1. Married persons. Separation & divorce.
   Psychological aspects
   I. Title
   155.6'43

Typeset by Litho Link Ltd., Welshpool, Powys, Wales.
Printed and bound in Great Britain by Courier International Ltd,
Tiptree, Essex.

Contents

Acknowledgements

For many years men and women, of all ages, have shared with me their experiences of life and particularly their journeys through separation or divorce. As a counsellor and agony aunt, I have learned from countless people of both the uniqueness and the similarity of those experiences. I owe each client and each correspondent much gratitude. Special mention must be made of Sally, Brian, Mary, Albert, Carl, John, Mary, Doreen, Michael, Peter and Debbie who will recognise their genuine contributions even though I have given them fictitious names. I am indebted to each one of them for their kind co-operation.

The Glossary of legal terms could not have been compiled without the very able assistance of Mr Alan G. Cooke MA (Oxon), barrister and Clerk to the Justices at Teesside Law Courts. His help was invaluable and sharpened considerably the clarity and precision of the definitions.

My colleagues, friends and family have always accepted me, even though they know I am a voyeur of human relationships. I have neglected them all during the writing of this book but I offer no apology, for their support, encouragement and trust have enabled me to get on with it!

Lastly, I want and need to thank Norman, my husband and partner, who has given me time, space and care throughout the production of this book. I am also ever mindful of the value of our relationship, which has provided an ample testing ground and a source of challenge thoughout the years.

Introduction

This book is for ordinary men and women contemplating, deciding on, or implementing the end of their partnership by separation or divorce. It is for those who have a marriage certificate and for those who have been committed to each other but who have no legal tie.

Splitting involves many practical issues, such as money, accommodation, possessions, and in many cases children. It also arouses intense feelings such as frustration, anger, resentment and rejection. Until these emotions are accepted and understood, it is hard positively to think through and make critical decisions. Therefore in this book there is equal emphasis upon facts and feelings.

The purpose of this book is threefold. The first aim is to help readers clarify priorities and face practical issues realistically. The second aim is to encourage the recognition, understanding and acceptance of the feelings encountered before, during and after the split. Thirdly, the book aims to promote the preservation of self-esteem, self-respect and confidence. Self-worth is the most vital ingredient when planning a new life ahead!

Endings can be abrupt or lengthy. Parting can bring relief and release as well as pain and insecurity. Each couple will find that they share some similarities with others breaking up but, as each individual is unique, much of their experience will also be very different and special to themselves. The important message is that each step or stage can be negotiated and adjusted so as to balance evenly the resolution of wants, needs and expectations of those involved.

There is no magic wand or palatable prescription for couples in conflict. However, men and women can emerge from separation and divorce with a will to fashion new lifestyles and create fulfilling new relationships. The whole experience needs to be seen as a challenge rather than a threat. The retention of dignity and self-respect is a key issue, and much of this book will promote self-awareness and positive thinking.

1
The challenge

EXPECTATIONS

When two people decide to live together, there is usually much anticipation and excitement. Alongside the pleasures and frustrations of practical planning, there run many idealistic visions of perpetual happiness and mutal content-ment. The couple want to please each other so as to ensure a chance to 'live happily ever after'. Their hope is that they can emulate the fairy stories, forget past troubles and settle to enjoy each other to the full. Even the most sceptical person is prepared to take the risk in the hopes of finding 'perfect harmony'.

Why do we have these expectations? A popular theory is that it is because we invest so much in the notion of romantic love. From early childhood we receive messages which shape our interpretation of the word 'love'. In the context of personal relationships this 'love' assumes magical or mystical qualities. We talk of 'falling into' or 'falling out of' love. This suggests the process is outside our control. It is unpredictable and we find it difficult to explain. Sally and Brian have lived together for six years, and this is how Sally remembered the beginning of their romance:

'It was wonderful when we first met. As soon as he walked into the room I knew we were meant for each other. He looked across at me and, as our eyes met, I realised instantly that he felt the same way. It was love at first sight and it was a tremendous feeling.'

Mary and Albert have been married for nearly 50 years. They both remembered the start of their courtship:

'It was love at first sight for me . . . but I was too shy to tell him!'

"I was more interested in her older sister at first . . . and then one day, right out of the blue, it hit me. That was a big moment in my life, I can tell you.'

We also talk of Mr and Mrs Right as though some unknown outside force determines a match for us. Many men and women see life's ultimate goal as finding this pre-ordained person. Carl has never had a serious or lasting relationship with a woman. He explained his single status as follows:

'I spent my teens and early twenties in searching for knowledge. I believed qualifications and a good, steady job were passports to happiness. I was wrong. I should have searched for my soulmate. I now realise my Mrs Right is probably unhappily married to someone else. I have tried all ways of looking for my ideal woman in recent years but I have left it too late. Perhaps she died of cancer or was killed in a road accident. I will keep on looking, but there isn't much hope.'

Another common belief is that 'love' is some kind of insurance which will protect and preserve us whatever happens. It is as though we see it as some kind of cocoon or cushion which will deflect pain and hurt so that we are troubled no more. Messages of this kind are transmitted to us all the time from various sources. 'All You Need Is Love' is the title of a Lennon and McCartney popular song. Bertrand Russell said, when referring to people who married because they were in love, 'each imagines the other to be possessed of more than mortal perfections and conceives that marriage is going to be one long dream of bliss . . .'.

The two couples mentioned Sally and Brian and Mary and Albert, talked freely of the dreams they had before setting up their homes. They admitted to using romantic love as the prime criterion when they made their decisions. They had short-term fantasies, one of which was how they would spend every spare moment together. Longer-term day-dreams visualised a lifetime of mutual support and comfort. They felt intoxicated by the uniqueness and exclusiveness of their relationships. The time they had spent together previously had enabled them to reveal to each other their most attractive and interesting characteristics. They displayed excitement and an eagerness to get closer to each other. Each partner had a genuine desire to be united.

They are ordinary people, and countless couples begin their partnerships in very similar ways. It is a step in the dark, but there are high expectations that the gamble will prosper. With 'true love' and a bit of luck, their future is ensured.

Everyone has their own personal picture of this mysterious and indeterminate force called 'love'. If we have never experienced it, we feel denied or deprived. When we lose it, we grieve because we feel empty and bereft. We feel happy and content when we have it. It is often the most important influence in our lives. It is something we expect will change our lives and bring us happiness and fulfilment. We see 'love' as the passport to contentment and attachment.

REALITY

Expectations, however, require some action if they are ever to become reality. After the first flush of euphoria, the humdrum round of everyday living descends. Each partner becomes more relaxed and lessens the need to sift words and actions. Both become less inhibited and reveal their true selves much more frequently as the relationship becomes safer. As the closeness develops, there is an inevitable dicovery of previously well-hidden physical and character blemishes. Learning to adapt to your partner's bad habits and getting him or her to accept yours often requires tolerance and adaptability. Shame, regret, remorse, humiliation, anger and frustration are uncomfortable feelings. It is often hard to share these and other strong emotions. If they are stifled, however, they tend to burst out in an uncontrolled and frequently destructive way when we least expect them.

Once a couple are living together, each partner becomes increasingly aware of the investment, responsibility and obligation required. This awareness usually begins when, as individuals, the couple take up daily living again and get involved in the outside world. Instead of responding simply from a position of their own wants, needs and fears, they recognise that now they have to ascertain and consider the wants, needs and fears of their partner. Sometimes there is no difficulty as these will coincide, but more generally they will differ and some negotiation will prove necessary.

Sally and Brian explained how they accidentally and painfully found that their commitment to each other varied:

'We had been together for about six weeks. Brian followed me in from work and together we were preparing a meal. We were chatting casually when Brian mentioned that he would be away the next week. He told me that he had volunteered to go on a two-week training course and that he would not be coming home for the intervening weekend as he was taking the opportunity to visit friends in the area. He was full of it and naturally very excited. I was furious! How dare he make this decision without any reference to me! I felt slighted, ignored and undervalued. I seethed, and it had to come out.'

Brian gave his reactions:

'When Sally attacked me I was dumbfounded. I hadn't expected that kind of reaction and I was caught off-guard. We got locked into one of those mindless rows where you go from attack to defence and back again. Once it got going it was frightening because we didn't know how to stop.'

Sally continued:

'He said some brutal things and I felt he was a complete stranger. He was nothing like the man I loved.'

Brian went on:

'She eventually burst into tears and slammed out. I thought I had lost her. I felt I had let myself down by being thoughtless and that she would reject me now because she had seen that previously hidden side of me.'

Sally concluded:

'I never trusted him in quite the same way again. I realised he wasn't as committed to me as I wanted him to be. On looking back, I now see that I withdrew some of my commitment to the relationship that day.'

These kind of revelations can happen at later stages in the relationship. Mary and Albert became aware of their differing investments in their relationship at various times in their marriage. They highlighted one time when they both learned a great deal about themselves and each other. They had been marrried for more than five years when Albert was called up and went to serve as a soldier in World War II. He was away almost seven years, with rarely a chance to go home on leave.

Mary remembers that time very vividly:

'When Albert went I felt that I would never cope with the responsibility. We had two young children and we had become very dependent upon each other. There was little money and times were hard. I kept myself busy and made sure we were clean, fed and warm. There was no way I would go with some of the other women chasing a good time. The first time Albert came home on leave I was very excited. . . . When he told me that he had been to concerts and out drinking with the lads I was furious! How could he, when we were living hand to mouth at home?'

Albert took up the story:

'I was stunned when she rounded on me. It wasn't until months later that I realised I had taken her for granted. Her devotion to our children and home had outshone mine. It had never crossed my mind that I was being selfish. I was ashamed when I realised that she had refused the chance to go out and enjoy herself because of her commitment to me and to our marriage.'

Mary remembered the feelings:

'That was a terrible leave! When he went back I wept for days. Some of it was because I missed him so much, but most of it was because I had lost something. It was my naivety! In my own simple way I had expected Albert to give to the marriage exactly as I did. For the first time I began to realise we were different. I also recognised that sorting out the commitment to the relationship was complicated. We talked a lot about it many times. We often remember and try not to make assumptions, but we still make mistakes!'

Responding to each other is important, and each couple has to find their own particular patterns of communicating and sharing. They have to be aware that the one union contains two relationships: his and hers. It is necessary to look at issues from both points of view. It may not be possible to satisfy both partners, but if each is heard and considered fairly then there tends to be less discontent.

Some men and women prefer to live in a land of make-believe. They ignore and avoid facing up to reality, and either put their partners on a permanent pedestal or reject their partners' humanity and finish the relationship quickly so that they can go and chase their dreams. Either way prevents them from having an equal relationship, because they feel either inferior or superior. Accepting the reality of loving, which includes discipline, concentration and patience, doesn't happen automatically. 'Is love an art? Then it requires knowledge and effort,' writes Erich Fromm. Perhaps this is a key problem, in that we mistakenly believe love is spontaneous and inevitable. The reality involves work!

OUTSIDE INFLUENCES

Whilst a relationship is unique, both partners have to interact with the outside world and this can have a strong effect upon the relationship. Work, holidays, friends, family, in-laws, hobbies, interests, television, past relationships, children, religion, politics, money and ill-health are some of the outside influences which can either enhance or hinder a close personal relationship.

If we consider work, for example, we have little difficulty in recognising that it has considerable impact upon our lives. It normally occupies much of our time and concentration. The timetable of our day and week is often governed by our working hours. This work, whether paid or unpaid, determines our sense of usefulness. The lack of job satisfaction or sense of achievement can produce an overall sense of worthlessness. Promotion, deserved praise or a merit rise in pay all raise the morale of a worker. Unemployment, redundancy, demotion or feelings of being superfluous, inadequate or ineffective produce the reverse effect. Failure or insignificance at work can manifest itself as impotence in bed as well as a lack of confidence in general.

The status a paid job gives is also important. When you are

introduced to someone new, the first question is usually 'What do you do?' The generally accepted answer is a title which describes a paid job. This gives the listener three clues on which to build a judgement of you. The first is an indication of aptitude, skills and intelligence. The second is a notion of your social standing, and the third is a rough estimate of what your pay might be and therefore a guide to your financial standing. Once the questioner has some inkling about the job, he or she can then make judgements and assessments accordingly. How often do you hear someone saying 'I'm only a housewife,' or 'I'm between jobs, I'm afraid.' These are apologies and give insights regarding the speaker's sense of worth. Within a partnership a couple need to feel equal and valued by each other. If the messages from outside deny this, then it is difficult, but not impossible to restore the balance.

The sharing of the workload within the home is another very significant area which needs to be negotiated openly. Two adults require regular domestic maintenance, but if one partner is allocated the cleaner/shopper/cook role and the other the banker/decision-maker/organiser role without discussion, then they may soon feel either covertly powerful at one extreme or subservient at the other. All domestic arrangements are parenting jobs, and if they are not shared then the couple become one parent and one child in this context. Sometimes partners get locked into these roles and the struggle for equal adult status results in conflict. Successfully negotiating the balance depends upon the flexibility of both partners and their resolve to find their own unique pattern of division of household chores which suits them and allows them to feel valued. Overdependent and overbearing relationships are notoriously shortlived when the two partners want to be mature adults.

Work is one outside influence among the many previously listed. When troubles brew, it is hard to remember that there are these pressures around. Warring couples too readily accept responsibility or apportion blame to their partner. Much of the hurt and guilt stems from this common assumption that he or she is at fault. All sight of other contributing factors is often lost.

DOUBT

Just as it is normal to have wants, needs and expectations, it is also natural to have doubts and fears. We often deny or discount them but, if we are honest, we know our own frailties and we do take measures to protect ourselves. Doubts and fears rise to the surface when there are other painful issues around. They intensify and magnify, and it is important to remember that when we are in attacking or defensive positions we exaggerate all the bad points and conveniently forget anything good.

Trust is an essential ingredient in any partnership. We speak of 'investing' trust or 'betraying' it. We know almost instinctively those we can trust and those we suspect. We say, 'he or she is genuine and therefore we can trust them.' Some people are more worthy of our trust than others. When two people begin to live together, they take each other 'on trust'. It is not, however, a static ingredient but one which can fluctuate. The confidence, integrity and justice of the relationship depends upon the development of trust, and so it is a very delicate and vulnerable commodity. The process of giving and receiving an increased amount of trust places an additional responsibility and susceptibility upon each partner. As both are individuals and therefore differ in their capacity and rate of accepting and adapting to change, it is an area of possible conflict and pressure.

Sally and Brian had problems which stemmed from doubts. Brian arranged his fortnight away never doubting that Sally would accept this arrangement. Sally, however, reacted strongly because her doubts were her hidden agenda. She didn't know how far she could trust Brian. She had doubts about how much trust she should invest in the relationship, and one of her greatest unspoken fears was that Brian might betray her. This is how she explained it:

'My ex-husband was a salesman and he worked away most weeks. I used to feel sorry for him. He made me feel very guilty when he telephoned and said how much he missed me. He talked of lonely nights and cold, uncomfortable hotel bedrooms. He described solitary meals and expressed a great longing for me. Then, when it all came out about his girlfriend, I learned he had been taking her with him. She enjoyed telling me that she had witnessed those phoney telephone calls. As soon as Brian mentioned going away, it all came back. I had to protect myself. How could I trust another man? I had to be on my guard. Some would say I have a suspicious mind, but that is what life has done to me.'

Sally withdrew some of her commitment to the relationship with Brian that day. Her ability to trust had been so bruised in the past she felt unable to take any risks at that stage. Doubts about oneself and fears of being unable to rise to the expectations of one's partner also affect the well-being of the relationship. Sometimes one partner puts the other on a pedestal and refuses to accept the partner's humanity, as previously mentioned. This is a tremendous strain and usually ends in the 'perfect' partner producing some shocking or bizarre behaviour in an attempt to show the need to be accepted as he or she is.

Different standards of personal hygiene, citizenship, family loyalty, education and cultural or religious backgrounds, all of which shape us into what we are, create doubts. There is a need to review all standards and beliefs so that each partner is aware of the attitudes of the other. Both partners are entitled to their own codes of conduct and moral obligations, but they need to make sure that their partner understands why they have those beliefs and principles in order to tolerate them.

All doubts and fears need to be acknowledged and aired. We need to check their validity as we often create more fear because the source of our doubts is unknown and it is the unknown which we fear the most. Doubts are signals which tell us that there is some unfinished business around which needs to be clarified and checked out.

CONFLICT

Conflict is part of every human experience. Most of us fear it and yet we meet it at home, at work and in our community.

The media constantly bring us reports of conflict in our country and throughout the world. Though we would like to lead quiet, peaceful lives, the reality is that conflict arises from our different opinions, values, desires, needs and habits. These differences are most frequently found in close personal relationships. Only dead relationships can boast absolute harmony!

Much progress in the world, throughout the ages, has come about as a result of conflict. We can see the positive benefits when it is handled skilfully, as in a sporting competition for instance. Competitors need to challenge each other and aggressively strive to win or break records.

The disruptive and often destructive aspects of conflict disturb most of us. We have great difficulty in resolving contentious issues. Some of us avoid conflict at all costs and others deny it. It is sometimes used manipulatively in relationships in order to keep one partner either dominant or submissive.

When conflict is delayed or suppressed, it grows and expands until eventually there is an explosion when both partners can no longer control their strong emotions. They use words as weapons in an attempt to display the strength of their feelings, and often regret this later when their partner has taken the words literally and not recognised their use to ventilate feelings as a kind of letting off of steam.

Conflict within relationships can be divided into two parts. The first part involves the facts. These may focus around what the partner has done or omitted to do; on disagreements over policy issues such as money management; on differing practices, particularly involving trust, such as fidelity; and on incompatible expectations regarding roles or the use of resources (sharing one car is a good example).

The second part of conflict concerns the emotions. Some of the very strong and common feelings aroused are as follows: anger, mistrust, suspicion, defensiveness, scorn, resentment, fear, rejection, malice, frustration, elation, success, self-righteousness, relief, power, triumph, jealousy. Usually several of these strong and hard-to-control feelings surge through us and take over. We lose all our inhibitions and, in order to express how we feel, words stream from us without restraint. The words are good tools for releasing the emotional energy, but they sabotage any rational communication. They are meaningless, ineffective and self-indulgent. Unfortunately, the hearer often takes the literal meaning of the words to heart and is unable to see them for what they are.

Whenever deep feelings are aroused within us, our bodies seem to take over and produce symptoms which tell us that our instinctive physical defence mechanisms have sprung into action. These symptoms include trembling, sweating, a dry mouth, rapid swallowing, palpitations, hot flushes, muscle spasms, uncontrollable laughing and sobbing. Many people are unable to contain their restlessness and need to pace up and down or bang about. It is at this point that some resort to physical violence, especially those who cannot express themselves by words. The charge of primitive, instinctive, survival-seeking energy reaches explosion point as our bodies react biologically. It is impossible to think clearly, and concern or consideration for the partner (who is now the opponent) quickly disappears.

If conflict is to be resolved, then emotions must be dealt with first. Acknowledging the feelings and the physical reactions of the body is the first step. The next is to do some simple breath-control exercises to relax the body and restore some biological order. The thinking processes will then return quickly and the feeling of being in command, of self-control is restored.

Once your physical state is back to normal, treat your partner with respect and listen to the words spoken and the music behind them. Once you have listened to his or her side, state your point of view as calmly and carefully as you can. There may be a need for further clarification, but hopefully the whole situation will be calmer by this time and a compromise can be reached. Even if your partner refuses to offer you respect or a chance to speak, you will feel better because you will not be hampered by guilt or self-reproach.

Many relationships deepen and become more rewarding once both partners have learned how to work through to the other side of conflict. There are many rewards in making amends and experimenting in how to apologise, forgive and forget. Many people, however, cannot cope with conflict or survive permanent hostility. They do not recognise that they have a choice of either working through it or allowing it to damage the relationship and themselves.

John and Mary lived together for just over three years. They were both divorced from their previous partners and they had agreed to postpone marriage until they felt safe enough to make such a commitment again.

John, at 37, decided it was time to start a family. Mary was on the threshold of achieving her ambitions at work. She felt she needed to consolidate her career now that she was in her thirties. Her marriage and subsequent divorce had drained her of self-confidence and she felt her approaching promotion had been hard to win.

John was pleased for Mary but secretly felt threatened. Mary would soon have the larger income, and John viewed this with apprehension. His ex-wife had been a higher earner and she had flaunted her status, so that he had become demoralised and insecure.

Over a period of weeks, John hinted about a baby. Mary ignored his attempts to interest her and pretended not to hear. John got desperate and destroyed their birth-control devices. Mary was furious.

During the row both John and Mary hurled abuse at each other. They produced previously stored evidence of unreasonable behaviour, much of which was completely unrelated to the present incident. John became so confused by his anger and frustration that he lost his head and used his fists. All of those pent-up feelings had to burst out of him, and they resulted in uncontrolled and sudden violence.

Hurt and bewildered, Mary fled from the conflict. A friend accommodated her until she managed to find a room of her own. She explained later:

'I just couldn't cope. The relationship was lovely when everything was calm and smooth. Once we had a clash of opinions we couldn't handle it. I did my normal thing by running away. I just can't cope with conflict.'

Sadly, John realised too late that he always responded

hastily and before he could give his thinking powers a chance. His natural response was to become aggressive and vindictive if he felt he had his back to the wall. He shared some of his feelings about the break-up:

'I felt Mary lost all her respect for me and I got the contempt I deserved. I am left feeling inadequate and vulnerable. The only way I can survive is by keeping a low profile and licking my wounds. I fought like an animal. I felt like an animal, and she didn't deserve that kind of abuse.'

Both John and Mary feared conflict. They acted instinctively and without any framework. They needed help so that they could understand better their emotional and body reactions to conflict. They needed to work out some strategies for getting their feelings out into the open with more safety. They needed to reveal their feelings and ventilate the pressures at a much earlier stage, before these built up into explosive forces.

Wherever conflict exists, it can only be worked through if there are guidelines or pre-arranged plans to follow. Wars between nations, strikes at the work place, sporting fixtures (e.g. a boxing match) and other arenas of conflict normally have carefully worked-out rules or conventions which each side acknowledges and uses. Strategies and tactics are thought through and refined. If the boxer, for example refuses to adhere to the rules or the directions of the referee, he is criticised and penalised. In war situations there is outrage if conventions are not upheld. Similarly, in human relationships each party has to identify and then negotiate a fair set of guidelines for use in conflict situations. Otherwise it is too difficult to work through essential and normal differences without damage and hurt.

PARTNERSHIPS

Working partnerships contain two very different people. Both have wants, needs, expectations, doubts and fears when they enter the partnership. Their hope is that it will 'last for ever', and they feel a responsibility which is partly their own need to succeed. The other part of the responsibility is the burden which society creates by quickly and eagerly apportioning blame and pronouncing failure when a couple break up.

Living together makes two 'ideal' people into ordinary human beings. Tolerance and flexibility are often needed in abundance. Outside influences combine with individual habits, idiosyncrasies and character traits and affect the developing relationship. The couple need to explore and find their own patterns in order to learn how to laugh and cry together. They develop their ability to cope with conflict and increase their mutual trust and respect.

Couples have to go on working at their relationship, for as normal individuals they are changing all the time. The world around them is also changing, and they have to adapt accordingly. A living, vital relationship has ups and downs, strengths and weaknesses, and some good and some bad times. It is worth working through the problems with or without outside help if both partners can offer each other love, respect, trust and a sense of humour. If these basic ingredients are missing, then it is time seriously to consider parting before one or both partners becomes a victim or a casualty of the union.

2
The challenge – strategies and exercises

It is hard to think objectively when the emotions are involved. The following suggestions will enable thought clarification and will create some order so that rational assessments of the relationship can be made. Each exercise also offers positive strategies for working towards change. If both partners work through the exercises, either together or separately, it is an advantage, but they are still useful if only one partner is prepared honestly to face up to the issues involved.

Evaluating expectations

Look back to the time when you decided to live together or marry. Try to recapture your expectations and list them. Begin each item as follows:

'My *expectation* of this partnership was . . .'

When the list is complete, tick those expectations which have been fulfilled; underline those which you still hope to achieve; and cross out those which you no longer consider valid. You may have doubts or uncertainties about some, so leave those unmarked.

Now make a new list of your expectations of the partnership today. Begin each item with the words:

'My *expectation* of this partnership is . . .'

Once the list is complete, give each item some lengthy consideration. How realistic are your expectations? Can you sort them out into short- and long-term goals? What about your partner? Is it possible to share this exercise by looking at each other's lists and determining where you need to work? Also, take credit for your achievements.

Recognising reality

Roughly draw two dustbins and label one with your name and the other with your partner's name. List your bad points by putting them inside the dustbin shape and do likewise with your partner's bin.

Roughly draw two shop windows and again label them with your names. Put you good points into your shop window and your partner's into the other. This exercise works well if you do each other's good points and your own bad points! Sharing, discussing and amending can be fun.

Outlining outside influences

List all the influences in your life. These will include such areas as work or unemployment, friends, relatives, money, ill-health, politics, religion, etc. Draw a circle and allocate space to each of these influences to represent the size of

The here and now   *Hopes for the future*

impact or pressure they put on your life. How much space is available for you and your own self-maintenance, and how much is reserved for your partner? If you feel change needs to be made, draw another circle to represent how you would like it to be and start planning to implement those changes.

If your partner also completes this exercise, explore the possibilities of sharing and discussing the effect of your outside influences. Negotiating a change in priorities not only increases understanding but enables both partners to become more confident in communicating feelings.

Coping with conflict

How do you react when faced with conflict? Are your coping strategies consciously thought through, or do you react instinctively? The following exercises will help in identifying your present coping styles and encourage the development of a wider range of positive and objective strategies. The emphasis is on choice, because it is *your right* to choose how to respond, even if that choice is to do nothing!

Identify your normal reactions when you find yourself in conflict situations from the following list:

- ignore;
- deny;
- threaten;
- resist;
- attack (physically or verbally);
- challenge;
- block;
- retaliate;
- defend;
- submit;
- freeze;
- retreat.

If your style is not listed here, then try to put it into words and add it to this list. What can you learn from this? Are you an attacker, a defender or a procrastinator?

What emotions do you feel in conflict situations? Check through the following list and try to identify those which you feel when dealing with contentious issues:

- insecure;
- threatened;
- angry;
- frustrated;
- impatient;
- challenged;
- tearful;
- defiant;
- powerful;
- cornered;
- fearful;
- malicious;
- envious;
- self-righteous;
- overwhelmed.

What do you do with your feelings? Do you show them openly? Do you stifle them? Do you deny them?

Consider the following and decide whether you build either barriers or bridges in conflict situations. Barrier-building tactics can be:

Judging styles
- Criticising ('the fault with you is that you never listen to anyone!');
- namecalling ('what a stupid dolt you are!');
- diagnosing ('You only do that to salve your guilty conscience!');
- praising to gain advantage (inappropriately – 'You are so good with words. It is no use arguing with you!' or manipulatively – 'You are the decisive one, so I'll leave the final decision to you!').

Patronising styles
- Ordering ('Don't argue with me!' which implies you are superior);

- threatening ('Don't push me or you'll regret it!' This implies you are the stronger, either physically or characterwise);
- interrogating (questioning excessively in order to confuse, or questioning inappropriately in order to make your partner feel defensive).

Trivialising styles
- Diverting (switching conversation to other topics in such a way as to discount your partner's feelings or problem);
- logically arguing ('Don't get so het up! Let's stick to the facts and simply apply science!');
- over-reassuring or playing down ('Don't worry. It's just a storm in a teacup').

Bridge-building tactics can be:

Exploration
Getting to know the facts and the feelings by:

- listening (to the words and the music behind them);
- attending (taking in the messages of body language);
- interpreting (trying to feel *their* side, too);
- encouraging (making them feel you really want to know);
- clarifying (spotting and resolving misunderstandings);
- focusing (staying with the here and now. Make relevance the key word!);
- responding (being prepared to show how you feel and how their discomfort affects you);
- checking out (presumptions and assumptions often make for misunderstandings);
- understanding (this often means using both head and heart);
- explaining (giving your point of view honestly, in plain and intelligible language).

Goal setting

Making plans towards resolution without either party losing dignity or respect, by:

- assessing (looking at the facts and feelings and evaluating the present position);
- discovering (finding out all the options);
- challenging (creatively looking at ways of moving forward);
- planning (purposefully organising steps towards working through the problems);
- being realistic;
- being specific;
- strengthening and encouraging positive responses from your partner, and giving yourself credit for your own positive input.

Changing

Effecting change in yourself, your partner and circumstances by:

- adapting;
- developing;
- accommodating;
- evaluating progress;
- effecting action.

Erecting barriers increases suspicion; building bridges develops trust. How can you increase your trust-building strategies and decrease or abandon your suspicion-spreading techniques?

ABC of conflict resolution

A stands for antecedants. What was the background to this incident? Who was involved? When did it begin? Where did all the feelings come from? Why did it blow up now? How did it develop?

B stands for behaviour. What patterns of behaviour do you choose instinctively when you get into this kind of situation?

What about your partner? Can you predict his or her reactions?

C stands for coping strategies. These are to:

- acknowledge the body reactions;
- take deep breaths to restore physical order and increase oxygen to the brain;
- treat your partner with respect;
- be prepared to listen;
- insist upon your right to be heard and respected;
- state your point of view briefly;
- don't be sidetracked by old unfinished business;
- learn to eliminate loaded words (these often act to incense your partner and provoke more conflict);
- attend to the feelings first -- refrain from denying or ignoring your emotions and those of your partner;
- learn how to give and accept an apology.

Defining doubts and fears

It is often hard to determine the source of doubts and fears. Basic insecurity and life-experience can often inhibit confidence and assurance. Trust is a very delicate and intangible ingredient in any relationship. It is hard-won and easily destroyed. The following exercise will help to clarify the nature of your doubts and fears and their source.

Make a list of all your fears and then mark those which are directly linked with the partnership.

Make a second list of all the fears which stem from your partner.

Ask yourself the following questions:

- Are the fears real or imagined?
- Have you been aware of them for some time or have they appeared very recently?
- Are the fears constant or do they fluctuate?
- Do you have difficulty in trusting others or are your doubts new and entirely due to present circumstances?

- Are you sure they are not related to old and unconnected business?
- Have you doubts about yourself?
- How much do you trust your role in the relationship?
- What affects your self-confidence and self-esteem?
- Does your partner have doubts and fears?
- Do they correspond with yours or are they completely different?

If you feel overwhelmed by the doubts and fears, then do try to identify ways of bringing them out into the open, as the greatest fear for most people is fear of the unknown. Identifying and quantifying the doubts and fears helps to reduce the panic. Can you share them safely with your partner? Have you a trustworthy acquaintance who is a good listener and who is not emotionally involved? Why not consider sharing your difficulties with a marriage counsellor who is selected and trained to prompt people with relationship problems to think them through safely? Who else in your community can offer you confidential, non-directive help?

3

The decision

DECISION-MAKING

It is commonly assumed that the decision made by a couple
to separate or divorce is one single decision. The reality is that
two people are involved. They each make decisions in the
light of their own personal experience. They are influenced
by each other, but each considers what has happened and
how he or she feels in order to arrive at a definite opinion.
Sometimes the two decisions coincide, and together the
partners can then make plans for implementing the split.
Other couples find that they disagree, in that one wants to
part and the other wants to carry on. In the end, one partner
finds a way of imposing their will by force, persuasion or
other means.

Before any couple can arrive at a decision to part, they have
already made many other influential judgements. Once they
have arrived at the 'point of no return', and are ready to
acknowledge it, then many more decisions will have to be
made in order to complete the parting. The whole process of
breaking up requires frequent critical appraisal, culminating
in valid and often painful decisions. The preoccupation and
intensity of the whole process often puts great stress upon
one or both partners, as they gradually understand the
complexity of parting. The union has usually created intricate,
and often delicate, ties which need to be carefully and
systematically undone before the complete division is achieved.
Each step involves decision-making. People with confidence
and those much practised in making judgements have a
distinct advantage.

Another important factor is time. Some decisions are made
quickly and easily, whilst others require much thought and

heartsearching. One couple might make all their decisions over a period of hours or days, whilst another couple might spend months or years in working through from start to finish. The example of John and Mary given in Chapter 1 highlights the fairly rapid series of decisions, which began when John decided to force his need to father a baby and ended when Mary found herself adequate living accommodation and adjusted to living singly. Many decisions were made during a period of three to four weeks, and sometimes relationships break in a similar way. The majority of couples, however, take a much longer time to work through the process. Doreen and Michael shared their experiences.

Michael set the scene:

'I realised I was bored with the marriage after about five years. It had been a shotgun wedding and by that time we had a second child. Doreen was wrapped up in her children and her family. She was very close to her mother and sister, and with hindsight I now realise I resented this.

'I had drifted into making my own social life. I got involved in sporting activities and I ended each day at my local pub. I spent most of my time out of the home, and Doreen and I had little to say to each other.

'One evening a friend introduced me to his sister. She was very warm and attentive. Within a few weeks we were having an affair, and when Doreen found out she wanted to end the marriage. After a lot of heartsearching we both realised that it would be financially suicidal to part and the children would be the principal sufferers.'

Doreen took up the story:

'I knew our relationship was all wrong. We started our life together with a big disadvantage. I thought he married me through fear and at the direction of our parents. I always believed he would not have married me if he had been given a real choice.

'When I heard from a neighbour about the affair I was very angry. I felt cheated, because I was working hard to provide a good and caring home for our children. I thought we both shared that aim, and the affair threatened to shatter their security. My first reaction was to show him the door, but as we tried to think through all the possibilities, the children's welfare took priority. We decided to live under the same roof and be good parents until the children were old enough to be independent. Our very poor marriage ended then, and we became two parents for the next 15 years.'

Michael concluded:

'It was a long, slow business and it drained me of all my confidence. My affair had to end, and I didn't get involved with anyone else until the divorce was absolute. Even then it was hard to sort out a future with the children. Problems arise at Christmas and holidaytime because our children have to choose which one of us will get their visit. I expect it will get better eventually, but it does seem as though the decisions will go on forever.'

For Doreen and Michael the first decisions were when Doreen decided to invest her time and attention in her children and relatives and Michael decided to involve himself in out-of-the-home activities. It ended, more or less, when both Doreen and Michael adapted to living in separate accommodation, although it is clear that some bits of their joint business are still not resolved. Their choice to wait until their children were adults meant that it took years to work through their particular journey to eventual separateness. Perhaps their first decisions were made without any idea of the future implications.

Throughout their years of drifting towards an end, they made both great and small decisions. They found it impossible to pinpoint the most critical choice they had to make. Sometimes the behaviour of one forced the other to respond; at other times people or circumstances prompted the decisions. In some instances the choices were made quickly and even spontaneously. More complex judgements were thought through in depth over a period of time. Doreen and Michael made individual contributions to a series of decisions which formulated the route they followed until their separation and divorce were complete.

Making decisions can be complex in any life-situation. Men and women choose from a variety of options the most appropriate response in any situation. Sometimes a quick, intuitive or spontaneous choice is made. At other times it is necessary to agonise over a long period of time before arriving at a final judgement. It is hard to make up your mind when you are uncertain about the outcome of any decision made, and individuals often choose to do nothing without realising that they have made a choice!

The whole process is both demanding and draining. All too often the stress involved is underestimated or ignored. In most instances of separation and divorce, the choices are not made lightly. As we have seen in the cases used earlier, each partner tries to determine what is required in the light of the circumstances and the people involved. In the end, most men and women attempt to find the path which will give them the least trouble, but finding that path is far from easy!

WHO MAKES THE DECISION?

From the point of waking each morning, the average person makes many decisions during the course of a day. Some of these decisions are completely personal, whilst others affect one or more other people. Many of the decisions we make entirely for ourselves; some we make jointly by negotiation; and other decisions are made for us either with or without our agreement.

The judgements we have to make vary in the degree of simplicity or complexity. We make short-term decisions such as what we might eat or drink, medium-term decisions like planning a holiday, changing job or moving house; and longer-term decisions such as making a will, taking out an insurance policy, or investing in a pension scheme. The difficulties encountered when deciding to split from one's partner result from having to make so many decisions of varying complexity and future implication. The volume of judgements waiting to be made is a very real pressure. Most partners dread tackling all the issues, and this is because the three great fears are ever lurking in the shadows of the mind. These are fear of the unknown, fear of failure, and fear of change.

In other areas of life, decisions are made by people who are given or assume the right to make them. There are those who make decisions because they have most power and authority. These include politicians, judges and leaders. Some people are given jobs with the responsibility of decision-maker as part of their job description. Managers, administrators and parents fall into this category. A third group of decision-makers are those who have most knowledge and expertise in a particular field. Surgeons, doctors, engineers and craftsmen are good examples of this group, as they all make a diagnosis and determine treatment based on their knowledge and skill. The fourth and last group of decision-makers are the person or persons most intimately involved and affected by the outcome of the decision.

When a partnership disintegrates, there may be some conflict regarding who should make the critical and essential choices. Sometimes the role of decision-maker is seized by the most powerful partner and this is seen as a very aggressive act by the other partner. Some partners feel they are the most responsible, in that they may have made most of the partnership decisions previously. In some unions one partner feels that he or she is more able to see and understand the wants, needs, expectations, doubts and fears of *both* partners, and therefore insists that he or she should take the initiative. When the partners are prepared to base their decisions upon the involvement of and affect upon each other, they can usually negotiate and make a more equal job of their decision-making.

When decisions are imposed upon us by someone who assumes authority over us, we feel very submissive. His or her acts are aggressive and deny us the right to participate. We feel devalued, inferior and underestimated. In many instances the greatest reaction is anger. If there has been a denial of equal rights in the decision-making, then there is often an added sense of hopeless resignation. When one partner forces his or her opinions, views and judgements upon the other, there are always strong and lasting feelings of resentment, which ultimately turn to bitterness. Some of the anger is often self-criticism, in that the submissive partner feels he or she ought to have been more aggressive.

The division of responsibility in a partnership is a key issue when the couple want to split. If one partner has previously taken charge of all the administrative bits of their life together, such as banking, paying bills, writing letters and similar chores, then that partner frequently feels that he or she is the key decision-maker in the partnership. It may be that one partner is allocated most of the practical roles whilst the other does the clerical and financial business. The less-practical partner may feel that it is within his or her role to decide the key issues because of his or her familiarity with paperwork and the more official business of the union. Again, the partner denied the chance to state his or her preferences and be part of the decision-making process is left with feelings of being belittled and put down. These feelings are added to the general discomfort of the situation and increase either the guilt or sense of failure.

It can be infuriating when a partner assumes he or she has special knowledge and is determined to make all the decisions because he or she 'knows best'. Such a partner usually claims to know all the facts and refuses to listen to any attempt at modification or amendment. The diagnosis is seldom more than a manipulative ploy to secure his or her own choice of result. When the diagnosis has been made and the decisions are completed in the light of the one-sided interpretation, then the other partner is left feeling incompetent and very demoralised. The negative or bad feelings persist, as the opportunity to work at a fairer share of consideration is rarely achieved.

Sometimes one partner is very aware of his or her own wants and needs. That partner also knows his or her own doubts and fears. If he or she then chooses to concentrate on his or her own preferred results, the other partner is left feeling ignored and sometimes depersonalised. The other partner feels he or she is being treated as an object without rights or feelings. One partner may pretend to listen to the other side but in the end resort to a self-motivated decision. Avoidance, ignoring or placatory responses leave the other partner feeling unequal. The sharing of the decision-making by negotiation and respect for each other's point of view is the least devastating way at arriving at the resolution of critical and key decisions.

Everyone has the right to judge their own behaviour, thoughts and emotions. They also have the right to take the responsibility for the initiation and consequences of these upon themselves. They also have the right to offer no reasons or excuses to justify their behaviour. If everyone is their own ultimate judge, then there is no need to explain the reason for their behaviour to anyone else so as to be judged either right or wrong.

No partner is obliged to seek approval from the other for everything he or she does or says. The notion that partners are responsible to each other for their actions reduces their individual role to that of subordinate. A partner can offer information and explanation, but to feel obliged or compelled to seek justification or condemnation is degrading and humiliating. At such times there is little credence given to respect, and the result is usually more mistrust and distress. As a normal human being, a partner has a right to change his or her mind and cannot be expected to remain constant in thought, word and deed. There is no need for apology or recrimination for changing. Any person who is living is changing all the time. Raking up old misdemeanours and quarrels is out of order, as each incident ought to be dealt with at the time it happens. Memories are fallible, and it is unfair to fuel the fire of conflict with old and untenable garbage which has been rotting deep inside for too long.

Anyone can make a mistake, and most of us make them again and again. We have to take the responsibility for the consequences, however, and if we use that right, then no one can stand in judgement of us. The problem arises when one partner sees him- or herself as the 'goody-goody' and the other as the 'demon' or 'fool'. Polarisation quickly develops, and one partner becomes the injured or wronged party whilst the other is castigated and ostracised for being bad or wicked.

When important life-decisions have to be made, there is no shame in saying, 'I don't know,' or 'I don't understand.' Pressure is often put upon one or both partners quickly to

make up their minds. Each individual has to sort out for him-
or herself a decision which not only sounds right but feels
right. Each partner must be given enough time and opportunity
to make his or her decision, even if in the end that decision is
to accept a compromise in order to respect the fact that two
people are involved and each have equal rights and a
separate future ahead.

When decisions are felt to be critically important, other
people and outside pressures suggest that the only answer
lies in logical thinking. As ordinary human beings, we cannot
expect to be logical all the time. In times of conflict there are
so many deep and uncomfortable feelings which cloud the
mind and affect our ability to think in an orderly way. We
have a right to be illogical as we make our decisions. A gut
feeling often has no logical explanation, but when followed
rarely lets us down.

Many people have difficulty in saying 'no'. We feel a great
need for continuous approval, and believe that refusing to
agree will bring disapproval or criticism. When one partner
feels like this, he or she is at a great disadvantage, for the
other partner can abuse or manipulate for his or her own
gain. We have a right to say 'no' and a right to remain firm.
Attempts to bully, browbeat, cajole, ridicule, persuade or
barter are self-rewarding tactics and need to be seen as
methods of denying the right to choose without fear what is
felt to be the right response.

Decision-making is demanding, time-consuming and
disturbing. It needs time, patience, understanding, respect
and self-awareness. It is necessary sometimes to find
someone who is not emotionally involved and who is
prepared to listen whilst we think aloud. A marriage
counsellor is trained to do this and offers a non-judgemental,
accepting and confidential approach. Working through it all
with a counsellor also gives an opportunity to rehearse what
needs to be said and helps the less confident to communicate
more openly.

Arriving at decisions can be unnerving, but once the
choices have been made there is relief and a sense of
achievement, provided both partners feel their rights are still

intact and not violated. The decisions surrounding the partnership need to be made by both partners on the basis of compromise or each partner having an equal share of justice in the decision-maker role.

The raw and painful feelings left after a split are often due more to the way in which the parting was implemented than to the losses involved as a consequence of becoming single again. If more attention was paid to looking at the decision-making process, and due regard was given to a more equal involvement in the decision-making, then both partners would benefit and would feel less aggrieved.

WHEN IS THE RIGHT TIME TO PART?

Once a couple have taken the courageous decision to end their partnership, then the next question is about the timing of the split. The issues involved are influenced by both the circumstances and the practical needs. Some of the decisions will revolve around practical matters whilst others will be affected by emotional concerns. In many cases practicalities take precedence and this leaves one or both ex-partners feeling powerless and impotent. When events and circumstances override personal feelings continually, the people involved lose their self-esteem and confidence, for the messages they are receiving are that their wants, needs, expectations, doubts and fears don't count.

It sometimes happens that both partners want to implement parting as quickly and as cleanly as possible. Living together has usually degenerated to the state where any other mode of living seems infinitely better. A clean break is possible, but the criteria for this must include the adaptability of each partner both emotionally and practically. The management of dependency and independency within the partnership is critical, and where almost instant splits have been successful, there has been the retention of much independence throughout the union.

In many cases just one partner is in a hurry to make the break. This puts great pressure on the reluctant partner, and he or she often feels bulldozed or harassed into making plans. Peter told me of his stress when Debbie and he decided to part. His experience was very similar to many, and the feelings involved will be easily identified. Peter told his story this way:

'We had been together for over three years. During the past few months we had been too busy with our paid jobs. I had moved to a new department, and learning the new set-up absorbed me. Debbie had become the manageress of the hairdressing salon where she worked, and I thought her increased responsibility was getting her down.

'When Debbie told me that she wanted to move out, I was panic-stricken. She then went on to reveal that she had a new relationship and that she was going to move in with him as soon as possible. My first reaction was to hang on to her for as long as possible. I made every effort to prove why it was necessary for her to stay for the next few days. I pleaded with her to postpone her move until I could find a smaller and more affordable place. She remained firm and told me that a quick, clean break was best for both of us. I felt I had no answer and wasn't given any time to think it through.

'Within 48 hours Debbie had gone and taken with her half of all we had. I was left with a lot of practical problems, but they were insignificant when compared to the feelings of being rejected, discarded, and abused. My resentment turned to bitterness and my trust in human nature reduced considerably through this traumatic experience.

'I got my act together as quickly as I could in a practical sense, but I still haven't got over the feelings of being powerless and inadequate. It wasn't the break-up that caused most pain, it was the way Debbie railroaded me in order to get her way.'

Many people have great difficulty in finding accommodation when they contemplate parting. The first negotiation is whether it is practical for one of them to stay in the present home. Both partners need to see that each one of them requires time to organise amenable living conditions. This might be temporary, such as going to stay with friends or relatives, or long-term, as when taking on a lease. It is important to accept that their joint home is required as a base until definite and reasonably permanent arrangements have been made.

Money is another big problem. It may or may not be viable in a financial sense to split, and this will influence the timing of the parting. Where there are going to be economic problems, then the couple need to negotiate a more appropriate time to split so that both of them are free from any unnecessary burden. The key is in thinking it through and respecting each other's point of view.

Another determining factor can be health. Sometimes one partner has a health problem and needs the support of a carer in either the short or the long term. Finding a substitute may need some organising if the other partner finds it intolerable to perform the carer role. The healthy partner may need to stay until reorganisation is satisfactorily planned. This may provoke strong feelings of frustration, but once the break is implemented there is less likelihood of problems of intense guilt.

Paid employment is a big influence in anyone's life. Some jobs require a husband-and-wife team, whilst some couples work in the same environment by choice. When couples work side by side, there are added complications when they decide to part. Some consideration needs to be given as to how they can remain co-workers or, if they find this impossible, how they can delay splitting until one or both of them find employment elsewhere.

In the partnership where unemployment is a key factor, then special attention needs to be given to the questions of accommodation, money, health and feelings. The existing sense of failure and redundancy may be magnified. The practical and emotional issues often combine to reinforce the general sense of futility and hopelessness. Genuine concern, reassurance and understanding go a long way towards helping to raise morale. Couples in this situation need to talk about their feelings and bring them out into the open. If strong feelings are suppressed, then the usual result is depression. Preventive work, by talking, is the best way to avoid depression.

There are many things to be considered when deciding on the right time to split. Each couple will have their own particular set of personal needs and unique circumstances. Before a date and time are set, these issues need to be carefully addressed and negotiated. Each partner has a right to be heard and considered, and need not apologise or excuse his or her insistence on being given that right. When each partner listens and shares with respect, then critical decisions become less stressful and the right conditions for fair play ensue.

WHAT NEEDS TO BE DONE?

There are many practical tasks involved when a couple make the decision to part. Some of these tasks are the same or similar for both the cohabiting partnership and the married couple. The essential differences generally focus on the legal status of married couples, as they can only be legally free by divorce and the approval of the court. Partners without a marriage certificate are free to split without any legal formality at all. Some of the information under this heading applies only to separating or only to divorcing couples, whilst many of the less legally focused tasks explored will be common ground for all.

The safest immediate action is to get sufficient and sound legal advice. Concrete information dispels doubts, fears and fantasies. Facing up to reality is sometimes a very frightening confrontation, but facts do provide a firm basis for negotiation. Early consultation with a solicitor will determine whether the partnership can be dissolved without further legal help or if assistance is needed in the more complicated issues such as unreasonable demands or refusal to co-operate. A separating couple may derive comfort from knowing that, in a legal sense, the division of their property and possessions was correct, and a married couple may decide that they are sufficiently in tune, as far as making the splitting arrangements are concerned, that they can opt for a do-it-yourself type of divorce.

Other couples may wish to clarify issues such as agreements about finances and, in the light of initial legal advice, decide to secure the representation of a solicitor. If divorce is contested, or if one partner is uncooperative in any aspect of the terms of the divorce, then further legal help is essential.

The Citizens' Advice Bureau is very accessible and offers a free service. The workers are trained to give up-to-the-minute information in a clear, uncomplicated and precise way. Most town branches have a free extra service which enables a practising solicitor to give advice for up to half-an-hour. The CAB interviewer makes referrals by appointment, and these are usually at the CAB office. The address and telephone number of your local CAB can be found listed in the telephone directory, and are often included on the 'Useful Numbers' page. Libraries also have the address, telephone numbers and office hours of the local CAB listed.

Some areas have Law Centres, where staff are full- or part-time solicitors and free legal advice is offered to anyone in their area. Initial advice can be given on the premise that further representational help must be sought elsewhere. Again, details of this service can be found at the public library.

The Law Society also have a scheme which enables anyone, irrespective of financial means, to receive a short half-hour interview with a solicitor for a small 'fixed fee'. For £5 it is possible to get sound advice, but it is essential to specifically ask for a 'fixed fee' interview when making the appointment, as not all solicitors are included in this scheme. The CAB or local public library will let you see a list of local solicitors offering this service.

If as a result of an initial interview with a solicitor you decide you do need more legal help, then certain steps need to be carefully taken. The first is to ensure that the solicitor you choose is a specialist in divorce and related financial matters or partnership dissolution. A member of the Solicitors Family Law Association would be a reliable guide, as membership requires matrimonial lawyers to subscribe to a code of practice. A list of members in your area can be obtained from the secretary SFLA, 154 Fleet Street, London EC4A 2HX.

A second consideration is cost and how to get help if you are without sufficient means. It is reasonable to ask for some indication of the cost during your first interview. Your solicitor will be able to tell you of his or her hourly rate, and in addition there will be telephone and postal charges, any court fees including a barrister's fee if needed, and other possible expenses such as valuer's fees. Value Added Tax is also charged. As time is so costly, much discipline is required so that the interview can focus on unemotional, essential business. It is important to plan the interview beforehand in order to get the maximum amount of help in the minimum amount of time. The solicitor is not a shoulder to cry on or a general perpetrating a revengeful war! Your legal adviser has a duty to act in your best interests in the long term. Each partner, therefore, needs a separate solicitor, and this often causes animosity if within the partnership there has been a working relationship with one solicitor in the past.

Many men and women find themselves without money but still needing the advice of a lawyer. The Green Form Scheme is a help where divorce is simple and undefended, or when negotiating straightforward settlements. The solicitor carries out an assessment at the beginning of the first interview, if requested, and, dependent upon disposable capital and income, a Green Form application is filled in and signed. Two or three hours' legal advice and assistance may be granted to you, either free of charge or at a reduced rate subject to your particular circumstances. Each spouse is considered separately, so even if one partner is a high earner the other may still have an application granted. It is important to recognise that the solicitor will not be able to conduct your case or appear on your behalf in court under the terms of the Green Form Scheme.

When the legal business between splitting partners includes divorce-court issues such as maintenance orders, property orders, lump sum orders or matters involving children, then it may be more appropriate to seek assistance through the Legal Aid Scheme. Again, the solicitor will help by assessing your financial situation and by filling in the appropriate application forms. Once the application is sent off, you will be subject to further inquiry and asked to answer many searching questions regarding yourself, your home, your income and your savings, by way of a hefty financial statement form. If you have an employer, then they are also asked to complete a form. Once all the information is collected and considered a decision is made, but this often takes at least seven weeks. As work done by the solicitor *before* the granting of a Legal Aid Certificate is not covered by the certificate, there is often a prolonged period of inactivity until the decision is made known. The only exception is in cases of desperate emergency such as an application for an injunction, when a special pink form is used and is considered and granted immediately in the light of the urgency.

A decision to grant Legal Aid can either be to relieve you of any cost or you may be asked to pay a contribution calculated in accordance with your means. If the latter is the case, then you will be sent an offer setting out what you will have to pay and asking for your preferred method of payment. If you have capital you may be expected to pay a lump sum, but if your income is your source of cash then you will be asked to pay monthly contributions. In almost every case the monthly contributions must be completed within a 12-month period. A Legal Aid Certificate is not issued until after you have accepted the offer and made the first monthly instalment, or paid the lump sum contribution in full.

One serious misconception is that, once the Legal Aid Certificate is granted on present circumstances, there will be no further obligation to contribute. However, as the fees are paid by the taxpayer via the Legal Aid Fund, there is a need to recoup monies paid out from any monies or property gained by litigation. This means that someone granted Legal Aid will get legal advice and assistance without having to pay whilst the proceedings are in progress, but will be required to pay at least some contribution out of the final settlement. In matrimonial proceedings the first £2,500 of any property gained or preserved is exempt, as are maintenance payments.

Divorce proceedings follow a prescribed pattern whether you choose to conduct the business yourselves or engage solicitors to do it for you, provided there are no difficulties or complications. A step-by-step guide to simple divorce proceedings is included in Chapter 4. Intricate and contentious divorce proceedings require the expertise and dispassionate direction of lawyers. Issues relating to specific terms of the divorce can be explored with accountants and other advisers. The best advice is to find out as much as you can from every available source, so that you can make your decisions with knowledge and understanding.

Money is frequently a key problem when couples are about to part. Any joint bank or building society accounts need immediate attention. Branch managers normally have much experience of partnership break-up and they will not be shocked or condemnatory. It is vital that you let them know immediately, and that you negotiate with your partner a fair and just way of dividing any savings, even if only for a temporary period. Otherwise doubt and suspicion add to all the other negative feelings around. Negotiation is needed to ensure that no one feels cheated or short-changed.

Ongoing payments such as standing orders or direct debits also need attention. It is useful to list all payments and then organise a fair responsibility for future payments or cancellation. If one partner is remaining in the home, then decisions need to be made regarding the payment of outstanding accounts such as gas, electricity, general and water rates, telephone, hire purchase and rentals. How are these accounts to be paid in the future? You may have to make sure that the accounts are transferred to just one name. Will one partner need help with repayments for a short period until he or she has adjusted to living solo again? If you are able to manage, what about your ex-partner? The fact that you are splitting up doesn't mean that you have to refrain from being fair and compassionate. The fact that you are no longer partners doesn't mean that you are now bitter enemies!

A shelter is vital in our society. When couples part, one of the acute concerns is living accommodation. If one partner remains in the former home, the other is often confronted with the difficult problem of where to live. Sometimes short-term solutions, such as staying with relatives or friends, are possible. Some people find they have to go into hotel or bed-and-breakfast accommodation and pay dearly for it. Again, it helps if discussion and negotiation can take place. Short- and longer-term plans can be formed and independence gradually effected.

A partner remaining in the former home is also presented with many problems and decisions. If the accommodation is rented, then much will depend upon the tenancy agreement. If both partners are named as tenants, then each has the right to stay and neither can get the other out. It also means that both are jointly liable for the rent. If one name only appears on the tenancy agreement and rent book then there is no need for action, but if your ex-partner is the sole tenant you will need special help. The Citizens' Advice Bureau or your local Housing Department should be consulted.

Owner-occupied houses or flats present no problems provided you are the sole owner and you can continue with any mortgage payments. If the property is in joint names, then you are able to continue in residence until your partner gets a court order for the sale of the property. There are special circumstances which the court will take into consideration, but if one partner of a childless couple wants a sale the court usually orders it. The proceeds of the sale will then be divided appropriately between the two partners.

If ownership of the property is in the name of your spouse or cohabitee, you may still be considered as sharing ownership. A court may decide that your partner was holding the property in trust for both of you. You don't have to have anything in writing, but you do need to demonstrate that you have invested time, money or effort into improving or maintaining the property. Paying part of the deposit, sharing the mortgage payments, paying or doing repairs or improvements all count. It is good practice for both partners to keep records of such involvement so that fair apportionments can be made if the property is sold. A solicitor is advisable at an early stage where ownership and residence are in dispute.

Homelessness is very frightening to most people. Faced with such a prospect, panic usually takes over and fear and isolation cloud thinking. There are many sources of help in the community, and these need to be contacted without delay. Building societies often arrange a concession on mortgage payments when, for a short period of time, interest is the only payment required. If you depended upon your partner for support, then you may qualify for help through supplementary benefit, which can include mortgage interest payments and payment of general and water rates. If you are considering applying for help to the Department of Health and Social Services, then a useful interview with a worker at the Citizens' Advice Bureau or Law Centre is advisable. There are branches of organisations such as Shelter which specialise in helping people with housing needs, and also offer advice and information when there is the threat of homelessness. It is essential to get help before making decisions which may be irreversible.

Other necessary arrangements may include organising a personal passport, checking and possibly changing insurance, changing ownership details for a car and organising other car insurance cover, informing the AA or RAC with regard to change in membership, and effecting any necessary changes in membership details at social, sports or recreational clubs and organisations. Checking through personal documents and data is tedious and often upsetting, as the changes necessitated by the split make the transition from couple to single more apparent. It is much better to implement these tasks reasonably quickly and thoroughly, however, as the longer they are left the harder they become to complete.

Possessions can be neatly divided into three categories. Each partner will have some personal effects and the other items will be of joint ownership. If it is possible to have the joint possessions valued, it helps to share them out more fairly. However, sentimental value should not be eliminated, as sometimes this far outweighs any monetary worth. Again the emphasis is on open negotiation, with each partner respecting the other person's point of view so that personal preferences can be taken into account. Vindictive acquisition and one-up-manship may provide brief moments of self-gratification, but they fan the flames of animosity and invite criticism and censure from others around.

Many men and women hesitate before revealing to relatives, friends, colleagues and neighbours the fact that they have parted from their partner or spouse. Many have shared the fact that telling parents is often the biggest problem. The anxieties tend to focus on fears of being condemned and branded a failure, and risking rejection. The reality is that marital and partnership breakdown is now commonplace and everyone close is touched and moved by it. No marriage or partnership is sacrosanct. Normal people live within relationships, and a flavour of all the feelings that flow from the breaking of a union is felt by those around. Identification is normally the first reaction of family and friends, followed by an intense urge to protect the ex-spouse or ex-partner from further pain. When family, friends, neighbours and colleagues are put in the picture quickly, they can supply much support and stability at a time when it is needed most.

One of the hardest tasks facing the ex-spouse or ex-partner is launching him- or herself as a single again. It is hard to introduce yourself as a solo, but after the first few times it does become much easier. Sometimes rehearsing beforehand helps, because you can organise the words and this assists in conveying the message you really want to impart.

Many of the tasks needing to be done seem endless and frustrating, but if they are seen as achievements and planned as positive steps towards organisation and success, then each effort can be scored. The aim of this part of the progress through separation or divorce can be seen as a determined effort towards independence and, providing any necessary help and support is sought and accepted along the way, individuals can win through as victors rather than as survivors.

WHERE CAN HELP BE FOUND?

It is easy to offer help, but asking for it can seem a very daunting prospect. When couples are parting they often need information, objectivity, energy and confidence. It is not unusual to receive unsolicited opinionated advice, inappropriate recipes used by others in similar circumstances, pity, and the attention of voyeurs who thrive on the sordid details of other people's crises. The newly parted ex-spouse or ex-partner can become the focus of negative attention and gossip. The demoralising effect of this depletes any self-confidence or self-esteem which may remain after the trauma of the break-up. Suddenly all but a few loyal relatives and friends seem to be making false judgements and giving useless advice.

The human race can seem alien at this time, and this emphasises the separateness. Asking for help when trust in humanity is at a low ebb seems futile. It is important, however, to recognise that people can give a wealth of constructive help, information, advice and support if they have been specially selected and trained and have become specialists in the field of relationships and family problems. These workers need to use their skills and use them well in order to remain credible. Approaching the right door and asking for specific help is possible, and the result is worth the apprehension felt before making contact.

The help required can be divided into two main areas. The first is help with practical matters. There are several statutory and voluntary organisations which specialise in helping men and women with individual practical problems during and following separation or divorce. The Citizens' Advice Bureau, Law Centres, Women's Aid, refuges for battered wives and Social Services Departments are part of a huge list of agencies, as outlined in Sources of Help in the Community at the back of this book. Each area will have a selection of helpful organisations, and lists of these are usually kept at the local public library. Some Mobile Library Services have this kind of information prominently displayed in the van.

The second kind of help required is assistance in order to cope with and resolve feelings. It is natural to feel confused by all the emotion and inner turmoil, and some help is available. Close relatives, friends and colleagues can be a tremendous help, although they can also be too involved emotionally. This prevents them from being objective and their strong feelings sometimes become an added burden!

Agencies offering relationship and marital counselling often spend profitable time with separating people. The sessions focus largely on the identification of feelings and then on the understanding of them. This helps to create some order within the mind and encourages the ex-partner or ex-spouse to accept that his or her reactions are valid and in most instances justified. Many men and women have suspected some kind of mental breakdown, not realising that the pain, the anger and the guilt are normal grief reactions generally encountered by others in similar loss situations.

The principal need of anyone facing separation or divorce is strength to get on with it. Looking for people and agencies which can offer strength and support is vital if confidence and self-esteem are to be increased. Splitting needs to be seen as a challenge and not as a threat. The changes may bring discomfort at first, but working through in a positive and purposeful way with confidential and sensitive help is progress. Asking for help is a reaching out towards positive resolution. It may be the first and hardest step, but it needs to be taken. People with skills, knowledge, empathy and experience can only be effective if invited to help.

HOW CAN UNNECESSARY PAIN AND BITTERNESS BE AVOIDED?

In any relationship breakdown there are many losses. Loss of love and affection, loss of status, loss of trust, loss of a sexual partner and loss of a sense of belonging are just a few of the losses involved. Every person feels the loss of the life shared together and the loss of the plans and dreams made about the future. No matter how fleeting or lasting, there is always a sense of loss, a feeling of redundancy and some regrets about losing the special place that was held in the life of the ex-partner or ex-spouse.

Grief means pain, and many men and women ache and hurt when they face up to the reality of the ending of their union. Sometimes there are physical manifestations of the pain such as headaches, general debility, stress symptoms, stomach, bowel or bladder upsets. These and similar ailments are outward signs of that inner pain. A period of insecurity and uncertainty is often accompanied by a persistent feeling of being 'under the weather' physically. Many men and women complain that they 'lost' their good health at a time when they needed it most. Disturbed eating and sleeping patterns are often symptoms of grief. Worrying about finance or similar pressing issues prevents proper rest and a healthy appetite. Others find themselves withdrawing and feeling too tired to get up and face the day. Eating for comfort is another reaction in the grief experience.

Anger, guilt, frustration and remorse are all strong feelings, and they are all symptoms of the grief process. It is important to accept these feelings as justifiable grief and find safe ways of expressing them. Problems arise when strong feelings are projected and used inappropriately, and some undeserving person or situation takes the brunt. Suppressed strong feelings usually burst out eventually in harmful ways or fester as depression. You have a right to grieve, to feel sad and angry. It is normal and natural to be full of emotions. You also have the right to work through them and learn from them.

The first task in grieving is to accept the reality of the loss of the 'good' relationship and all the other losses involved. This may mean systematically listing all the areas of loss, and perhaps a close friend or relative can help with identifying some of them.

The second task is to accept the pain and recognise that the hurt will more than equal the love you invested in the relationship. It may hurt to remember the good times, but this is necessary because the memories will justify your involvement. There were many rewarding aspects of the relationship, and these need to be identified in order to reinforce your confidence in yourself.

The third task is to recognise that you now have to live without your ex-partner or ex-spouse. This adjustment is going to take time, and you need to set realistic goals or targets towards feeling agreeably independent. The world may seem barren or alien at first but remember, you have been single before! At any one time there are many other people living satisfactory and useful lives on their own. Always remember that it is a challenge and not an impossibility.

The fourth and last task in the separation or divorce experience is to find means of investing yourself in other ways. The investment you had in the relationship must be withdrawn, but it is extremely valuable and it needs to be reinvested elsewhere. Some people find new hobbies and recreational pursuits, others invest in study or training. If human beings are rather suspect initially, then look for safe ways of getting involved casually within relationships. The key thing at this time is to search for new and stimulating ways of getting involved with many people. It is a chance to explore and be adventurous. You have a right to extend your life, to search for new rewards and feel part of the human race again.

Self-respect, dignity, confidence and self-esteem are the ingredients needed when a man or woman struggles to rise to the challenge of the separation or divorce experience. The wise person will hold on to a positive evaluation of themselves at all costs. It is often difficult to dispel negative feelings at such a time, but it is vital to match self-criticism with at least one realistic pat on the back. One middle-aged woman once told me that her husband has complained about and criticised her for some months before they split. It had robbed her of her previously reasonable opinion of her capabilities and performance. When asked about her ex-husband's feedback to her in their 27 years of marriage, she instantly recognised that he had seemed well satisfied for nearly all that time, and had often praised her and boosted her morale until recent times. When she balanced the 9 or 10 months of criticism with the 26 years or so of appreciation, she had to acknowledge the fact that she had achieved much success for most of their time together. Similarly, men and women need to put recent troubles into context and accept and take heart from the positive contribution they made to the relationship.

THE FUTURE AND NEW RELATIONSHIPS

The most important person in your future is you! In order to enjoy life and find fulfilment, you need to be in good mental, physical and emotional shape. Following separation or divorce, many men and women feel totally drained by the experience. Acknowledgement of the effects is necessary so that plans can be made to increase total health and vitality.

Once all the immediate practical arrangements have been made, there is often time to take stock and evaluate. This is an excellent chance to look at your own potential and seek possible ways of investing it. Who are you? What are you doing with your life? Who would you like to be? How can you make plans to get nearer your ambitions for yourself? Self-development groups are a tremendous help at this stage, and they are often provided at Adult Education Institutes.

Physical health is very important. As an independent person you now have the responsibility for your own lifestyle. Eating, drinking, sleeping and exercise patterns need to be examined so that you can eliminate any over-indulgences and form good new habits. The discipline of caring for yourself will add to your feelings of achievement. This, in turn, will add to your self-esteem and confidence.

Relationships with others offer feedback and help to overcome unnecessary self-doubt and feelings of unworthiness. It is important to maintain old relationships and indeed to strengthen these. It may seem very hard to visit and share time with couples initially, but you do have a relationship with two people and each will be different. Lasting relationships will help at the present time and remind you that you have successful long friendships. It may be necessary to openly acknowledge the fact that such friends also want to remain friendly with your ex-partner. This will give you the opportunity to state your preferences, such as avoiding meeting initially if it is going to be painful.

New friends are a must! Newly separated or divorced people need to bring new people and new experiences into their lives. If this is not done, there is a void and a tendency to dwell on the past. If there is a local group of separated and divorced people, then this is good to join. By sharing coping strategies and ideas for the future, the members help each other to cope successfully.

It is sometimes essential for separated and divorced people to remind themselves that they are single again. There is often hesitation about developing friendships with the opposite sex. It is as though they need permission to begin thinking in terms of another partner. The reality is that many, many people get involved again and, because they have had the experience of relationship breakdown, they do benefit from that experience.

Finding potential friends, and particularly singles of the opposite sex, is often a problem. Singles clubs operate in many areas offering a weekly social event and sometimes group holidays. Some of these clubs have a host or hostess who meets new members and ensures that they don't sit alone. The local library may have details, and some clubs advertise in the local press.

Single men and women who need new challenges can often find stimulation and new friendships by joining study or hobby groups. There are many sources of interest in the community, and the newly single are at liberty to find out what is available so that they can choose a variety of purposeful activities. A common interest is a good basis for new relationships and meeting periodically, such as weekly, within the framework of the community centre, adult education institute or similar premises, ensures safety during the initial period of building up trust.

Shy men and women, who find it difficult to get involved in groups, often rely upon dating agencies or newspaper or magazine personal columns in order to meet possible partners. It is essential to make sure that the dating or matching agency is a member of the Association of British Introduction Agencies. In order to be a member the lonely hearts clubs are required to uphold minimum standards, and this goes a long way towards preventing exploitation and malpractice. Extra care is necessary when either advertising or replying to an ad in a personal column. It is not advisable to give your address or telephone number until you have met. A box number is the best answer for the advertiser and an address care of a friend is likewise for the answerer. Disappointment is prevalent, in that the replies are often unsuitable and the answerer is frequently ignored. This is often due to a surfeit of replies which overwhelms the advertiser. Meeting people in the natural, unorganised way is the most problem-free way of extending your social circle.

One of the positive effects of separation or divorce is the opportunity to get to know yourself! The changes in your life, which have stemmed from the split, will have helped to extend your flexibility and adaptability. You will have a clearer idea of what is important to you and what you need and expect from friends and relationships. You will have become aware of and identified fears and doubts about some parts of your responses within relationships, and hopefully will have begun to change and work towards reducing them. The new you will eventually be stronger and more confident. The loneliness, sense of failure and lack of self-esteem are as temporary as you determine them to be. You have the right to change your life and the right to choose and make it in your own style! By concentrating on the positive bits of each day and by giving yourself credit for getting through them, you will build a bank of confidence which will eventually enable you to make longer-term plans for a brighter future.

Separation and divorce mark the end of a chapter in your life. The beginning was full of promise, excitement and expectations. Some parts of the union are worth remembering because they were happy, fun and rewarding. It is good to keep these memories, for they are valuable. The hurt, the pain, the turmoil and bitterness will leave their mark. They have been difficult yet character-building experiences which have created the opportunity to explore the depths of your emotions and the heights of your coping skills. The old saying 'The deeper you love; the harder you hurt' is echoed by many men and women who have parted. The depth of the love is often reflected by the acuteness and length of the pain. Love makes us very vulnerable, but as human beings we need to share our lives and invest ourselves in loving relationships. We need to trust, to give and to receive, to enjoy the security of involvement in supporting, caring and offering concern.

The experience of separation or divorce affects each person in a unique way. It is an important happening which is intrinsically one of change. Each individual has the right to choose whether the effects induce threats or produce challenges. Perhaps the greatest comfort is in knowing that, just as there was a beginning, there is an end. Working positively towards that end is definitely an achievable goal.

4
The decision –
strategies and exercises

Are you a decision-maker?

For this exercise you need a pencil and paper and about an hour in time.

Think about yesterday and try to make three lists of all the decisions you made under the following headings:

- decisions you made entirely for yourself (e.g. the decisions to get get up, wash, eat);
- decisions you made jointly with others (e.g. arranging a time to meet or to share a meal);
- decisions which were made for you either with or without your agreement (e.g. the bank manager contacted you and refused to allow you to extend your overdraft).

Which list is the longest?

Which decisions gave you most problems?

Would you now change any of the decisions you made?

How often do you *decide* to do nothing without realising that you have made that decision?

Take another look at your lists of decisions and try to identify why you made them by using the following four categories:

- because you were in a position of authority and it was your right to decide;
- because you had been given the job to decide;
- because you had most knowledge and expertise;
- because you were most personally involved and affected by the outcome of the decision.

What have you learned about your patterns of decision-making and can you improve them?

Is the responsibility for the decision-making mine?

When change is necessary it is often difficult to determine which decisions are the sole responsibility of one person and which need to be made jointly. Sometimes one partner decides to seize power by making all the decisions. In other cases one partner abdicates his or her responsibility by putting pressure on the other to make all the choices. 'Let me know when you have made up your mind and I will fit in,' or 'I'll do whatever you decide,' are examples of this. The following questionnaire will help to clarify the situation and check out the areas of responsibility.

Questionnaire
- Who will be affected by this decision?
- Who will be most affected?
- Am I solely responsible for the outcome?
- Is the effect upon minors or fringe people (e.g. parents, friends) such that they need to be consulted?
- Is there a date and time deadline?
- Have I thought through all the options?
- Who will help me to think aloud with less emotion and reduced bias?
- Can I purposefully reject decisions which do not belong to me and push them back to their rightful owner?
- Can I suggest some ground rules for joint decision-making?
- How often do I recognise that doing nothing is a definite and sometimes valid decision?
- Do I give myself enough time and space to explore all the options?
- Do I ever give myself credit for making decisions?

Aids to decision-making

When confidence and self-esteem are low, it is often hard to make decisions. Uncertainty and insecurity magnify the doubts and confuse choices which may otherwise be simply and logically sorted out. There are two parts to this exercise. One part is to stimulate positive attitudes to self and the other part is to identify the principal criteria influencing the final decision-making.

Attitudes to self
Consider the following statements, and if you agree then either repeat them aloud or write them out in order to identify with them and internalise them.

- I have the *right* to choose my response. I can accept the decisions made for me by being submissive. I can choose to make all the decisions or refuse to make any, by being aggressive. I can determine which decisions are mine by right and those for which I share responsibility, and deal with them assertively. I have the *right*!
- I have the *right* to make decisions for myself, even if those decisions are the wrong ones. I have the *right* to make mistakes.
- I have the *right* to say 'I don't know.' I have the *right* to take time in finding out what I want. I have the *right* to make decisions in my own way and in my own time.
- I have the *right* to say 'no' without feeling guilty.
- I have the *right* to change my mind.
- I have the *right* to make my own decisions without the need to explain, excuse or justify my reasoning.
- I have the *right* to respect and be respected.
- I have the *right* to be heard.
- I have the *right* to be considered.
- I have the *right* to be free and equal in dignity. I have the *right* to use my reason and conscience with confidence.

Principal criteria in decision-making
Before tackling the choice of options when decision-making, try completing the following:

- I *want* ....
- I *need* ....
- My *expectation* is ....
- My *doubt* is ....
- My *fear* is ....

Each of the above will probably generate a list of wants, needs, expectations, doubts and fears. Listing them will help to sort out the best option.

Achieving progress

When a couple separate or divorce, there are many practical details to be attended to. The following checklists will help to ensure that all these details are considered.

Accommodation
Leased or rented property:

- Read through all documents carefully. (Check with local Shelter group, Citizens' Advice Bureau or Law Centre on any query.)
- Follow the instructions regarding necessary change of name with regard to tenancy agreement or lease document.
- Contact your local authority housing department if you think you might benefit from rent or rate rebate or if you feel a rebate needs to be increased.

Mortgaged property:

- Contact building society or other mortgagee if there is going to be difficulty in making the arranged payments. Most building societies allow mortgagors with financial problems to pay the interest only for a period of about six months.

- If the property is to remain in the hands of one of the partners and the payments are to be met in full, then there may be legal arrangements to be made with regard to the name or names involved. The manager of the building society will readily arrange an interview to discuss any detail and will supply relevant information. An informal discussion can allay fears and ensure mistakes are avoided.
- If the property is to be sold, then the mortgagee will need to be informed in due course.

Finding accommodation:

- Make a list of all the types of accommodation available, e.g. furnished rooms, bed and breakfast, unfurnished flat, hostel, hotel, sharing with family or friends, etc.
- Choose preferred and realistic short-term possibilities.
- Be objective about negotiations. If moving in with family or friends, make a firm verbal contract about payment, duration of stay, house rules, etc. If renting rooms or becoming a tenant, be sure to have references and rent in advance. Ensure you receive a rent book or receipt, a list of house rules, and a list of other tenants in the building. Check the fire and security standards and ask for information with regard to local services. Hostels and hotels will provide all the necessary information and supply any extra help if asked.
- Personal recommendation is usually the best help when trying to find accommodation. The local branch of the National Council for the Divorced and Separated may be able to offer suggestions. Newspaper and shop-window advertisements need checking out thoroughly. It is a good idea to take along a friend when viewing.

Once installed in temporary accommodation, then make plans for a more permanent home. It is hard to settle and build a new life before a long-term home is found.

Money

Trust is a scarce commodity when a couple part. It is very important to acknowledge this and act dispassionately. The following list will help prevent problems:

- Joint bank accounts – these need immediate action. Inform bank manager and, if possible, arrange an appointment together with your partner when you can close the accounts and make other arrangements. Similar steps need to be taken with other money deposits such as building society accounts.
- List all outstanding bills usually paid jointly. Seek negotiation with regard to paying them.
- List all standing orders, direct debits, regular payments such as hire purchase. Again, negotiations are required to determine responsibility.
- Check insurances and read the policies. Effect any changes which may have to be made.
- List any joint investments. Negotiate future plans.
- Value joint possessions and list them. Negotiate a fair and objective division.
- Change the name on regular accounts such as general rates, electricity, gas and telephone accounts.
- Close credit card accounts held in joint names.
- Arrange changes of name or names on joint membership cards, etc.
- A married woman needs to arrange to have a passport in her own name if she has previously been included on her husband's document.
- Inform doctor, dentist, optician, etc. if you have always been regarded as a couple. Facilitate change of doctor if moving out of the area. Your medical card explains how to do this.
- *advise relatives, friends and colleagues of the split now.*

They may be a valuable source of support!

Divorce by special procedure – a step-by-step guide

Step one
The spouse wanting the divorce asks for the appropriate form of petition and, if relevant, statement regarding the arrangements for children from the divorce county court office. Help from a solicitor may be obtained at any time for either advice on the grounds for the divorce or help with completing the petition.

Step two
The petitioner (the spouse wanting the divorce) lodges at the court office the following:

- the completed petition plus a copy for the other spouse. If the petition is based on adultery, then an additional copy is required for the named person;
- a certified copy of the marriage certificate;
- two copies of the completed statement regarding the arrangements for the children, if relevant;
- court fee. This is £40. Exemption forms can be completed at the court office.

Step three
The court office sends all the relevant copies to the respondent and any co-respondent in adultery cases. Notice of proceedings and an acknowledgement of service for completion is also sent.

Step four
The respondent has to return the acknowledgement of service within eight days in England or Wales (slightly longer elsewhere). Any counterproposals regarding arrangements for the children should be lodged at the same time. If a co-respondent is involved, he or she, too, has to return the acknowledgement of service.

Step five
If the acknowledgement of service is not returned, then the court office notifies the petitioner and suggests other methods of serving the petition.

Once the service of petition is returned, the court office sends a copy to the petitioner along with two other forms for completion. One is the form of request for trial and the other is the form of appropriate affidavit in support of the petition.

Step six
The petitioner completes the affidavit in support of the petition and takes it to a solicitor or court for swearing. The copy of the acknowledgement of service signed by the respondent (received from the court office at step five) or, in an adultery case, the signed statement of confession by the respondent is also required.

The petitioner also completes the request for directions of trial and deposits this at the court with the completed affidavit and other supporting documents.

If there are any previous court orders relating to the marriage or children, then these must also be included.

If there has been delay, in that the respondent or co-respondent has indicated intention to defend on acknowledgement of service but has not yet filed an answer, then the petitioner needs to wait 29 days after the service of the petition to the respondent and co-respondent if relevant.

Step seven
When the direction for trial is received, the registrar reads and considers the documents.

If all is in order the following actions proceed:

- The registrar certifies entitlement to decree and, if appropriate, any costs claimed.
- The court office arranges the date for the pronouncement of the decree by a judge and for his consideration of the arrangements for the children, if relevant.
- The court office sends the date or dates to both the petitioner and respondent.

If the registrar is not satisfied, requests are made for further evidence or information. This may be sufficient and the actions above are implemented. However, if the registrar is still unsure after further consideration, he may direct that the petition be removed from the special procedure list. A new application then has to be made which will result in a date for a hearing in open court before a judge.

Step eight

On the date arranged in step seven, a judge pronounces decree nisi. The petitioner and respondent need not be present. *The couple are still married until decree absolute is pronounced*, approximately six weeks later.

If children are involved, the judge will receive the parent with whom the children will live in his or her chambers in order to clarify and approve the arrangements. The other parent may also participate. The judge carefully considers these details. A court welfare officer's report may be required. The judge may refer the parents to the Family Conciliation Service in order to discuss arrangements for the children in a less formal atmosphere. Once the judge is satisfied, orders are made for custody and access.

Step nine

Six weeks and one day after the pronouncement of the decree nisi, the petitioner applies to the court for the decree to be made absolute. The form is available at the court office. It is necessary to have completed the arrangements for the children to the judge's satisfaction and certification.

Step ten

When the court office receives the application, the records are checked to ensure there is no reason for delay and then the court office issues a certificate making the decree absolute. A copy is sent to both ex-husband and ex-wife.

If the petitioner does not apply as in step nine, then the respondent can apply to have the decree made absolute after three months and six weeks of the decree nisi being made. The respondent needs an affidavit to support the application.

The court office then fixes a hearing and notifies the petitioner. On the date fixed, the respondent attends before a registrar who considers the application. If the registrar is satisfied, the decree making the decree absolute is issued and copies go to both ex-husband and ex-wife.

Divorce by special procedure can be stopped at any time if the couple are reconciled.

Contested divorce requires the skilled help of lawyers.

Divorce can be applied for after one year of marriage.

5
The children

There are many childless couples these days, now that successful steps can be taken to avoid having children. The majority of couples, however, still choose to have children, as they see the role of parenting as a very creative and fulfilling part of their being. The decisions surrounding the choice of whether to become parents or not often cause conflict in partnerships. When couples with children consider separation and divorce, there is a whole extra dimension of complications. It seems reasonable to concentrate specifically on the various aspects relating to children in this part of the book.

DECISIONS ABOUT HAVING CHILDREN

Before a couple begin to live together they need openly to discuss their views and state their desires with regard to having a child or children. Every partner is a unique being and needs the opportunity to share with his or her partner feelings about parenting. For some the decision is easy, and both partners agree in principle to plan for the time when they can accommodate a child in their lives and open their hearts and home to another person. Others, meanwhile, may feel that parenting is not for them. For some couples it is a source of conflict, in that they cannot agree. It is better to find out that there is this fundamental difference at an early stage. Successful compromise can be achieved, although rare. The basic need to parent can become obsessive and result in many regrets and resentments. It is far better to part and find another, more compatible partner than to live in hope that somehow the situation will change.

When a couple agree to avoid having children, they need to be united and form a policy which will combat the pressures from others, especially their own parents. Grandparenting is seen to be very rewarding and almost a right. When prospective grandparents feel thwarted, they put a great deal of pressure on the childless couple. This can lead to exaggerated in-law problems which may produce a great deal of tension within the partnership. Other relatives, friends and colleagues can be equally as critical, and it takes considerable courage to ignore the oblique comments and implied censure. With a worked-out strategy and mutual support the couple can keep to their own decision secure in the knowledge that they have thought it through and arrived at the right and unique decision for themselves.

The decision to have a child is more complicated for those couples who do not have a marriage certificate. The extra considerations have much to do with society's slowness, rather than reluctance, to change. Although there are many more couples living together, there is still some stigma attached to a child born out of wedlock. Illegitimacy is often allied to disadvantage and deprivation, even though there are countless examples to prove otherwise. The father is not obliged by law to support the child in the absence of a court order, but many couples find there is something extra to be gained with regard to commitment when the father gives his support voluntarily. The child can take the father's surname and, providing grandparents and other relatives make a will, the child can inherit.

Couples who desire children but find they are infertile are particularly vulnerable, and they need to be very open with each other. It is estimated that about 15 per cent of couples in Great Britain are affected by involuntary childlessness. There are many myths and misconceptions, and little credence is given to the deep effect it has on the personal and social life of the couple. In many cases personal grief and mutual misunderstanding drive the couple apart. Again, the message is talk and talk. The more we express how we feel, the better we are understood. As the possibility to adopt and foster decreases, the developments in artificial insemination, test-tube conception and surrogate mothering increases. Each remedy demands much soul-searching and decision-making. Partners need to encourage each other and support each other if catastrophes are to be avoided.

If a partnership or marriage is going through a tricky patch, it is sometimes a temptation to look for ways of cementing the union in an attempt to keep it together. It could be falsely assumed that a child would 'rescue' the relationship. This is shortsighted, as the change from a twosome to a threesome requires security and stability if it is to flourish. A baby is not a sticking plaster, and the increased responsibilities and time-consuming maintenance required for a child's well-being mean that the parents have rather less time and attention for each other.

The decision to have children or not is one of the most major decisions a couple need to make. Unwanted babies can be a focus of many negative and uncomfortable feelings. The availability of abortion produces a way out, but the decision needs to be a worked-out one rather than a panic reaction. Many relationships have floundered because the woman has made a quick and independent decision, leaving her partner feeling ignored and undervalued. Counselling is necessary before and, even more so, after the abortion. Unfortunately this is not always available, and women and their partners often struggle with remorse and consequent depression. The relationship is affected, and the couple may need specialist help in coming to terms with their feelings and the effect upon the partnership.

It is important to remember that people do change, and so any major decisions need to be reviewed from time to time. The key is to communicate not only the words but the feelings behind them. Any major changes in health, job prospects, financial status, emotional or mental stability, dependency of other relatives and other circumstances will influence any major life-decisions, so a periodic checking out is both necessary and worth while.

STAYING TOGETHER FOR THE SAKE OF THE CHILDREN

When a wanted child is born, a new dimension is brought to the relationship of the two partners. They have created a new being, which is both a joint achievement and a joint responsibility. As parents take on their role as guardians, parenting pleasures and obligations follow. Some of these experiences will be shared between a couple, whilst others will be divided between them.

The new baby has three influencing relationships in his or her life: that is, the bond with the mother, the bond with the father, and the relationship with mother and father united as parents. When the parents split, some couples are able to keep the mother/child and father/child bonds stable and secure whilst their united relationship disintegrates, and in these cases the child is affected to a small degree. The majority of parents find this very hard to do, and agonise over the effects that separation or divorce will have upon their own personal relationship with the child. It may be relatively easy to leave a warring partner but nigh on impossible to leave a beloved child.

For many parents the responsibilities and obligations of parenting far outweigh any consideration of their own individual feelings. Many desperately unhappy men and women stay together for the sake of the children. Many marriages exist solely because of the presence of children. Each partner openly or secretly waits for the day when the youngest child reaches school-leaving age and he or she can leave with a clearer conscience. Such couples very often unwittingly burden their offspring with guilt, for the children are painfully aware that, but for them, both parents would have a chance of happiness elsewhere.

The factor which needs to take precedence over all others is the emotional wellbeing of each child in the household. Security, as far as a child is concerned, means a happy environment rather than financial stability. People are more important than possessions to a child. It is a well-known fact that a very young baby somehow recognises the mood of his or her mother. If she is agitated or angry, the baby is unlikely to be quiet and content. From very early on, a child picks up unspoken messages and is influenced by them. Disturbed and uneasy parents have disturbed and uneasy children. An atmosphere of antagonism or resentment is uncomfortable, and no amount of money or possessions will restore a child's equilibrium whilst the bad feelings of his or her parents zoom around. The child senses the discord and will interpret the raised voices, verbal abuse and physical violence. He or she is filled with unidentified fears, unless of course it is the normal behaviour of the household and he or she knows of no other.

When a child is perplexed and confused by the friction between parents, he or she becomes tense and begins to display unusual behaviour. Sleeping and eating patterns can go haywire, and soiling and wetting can sometimes occur. Young children display their regression by thumb-sucking or biting. Children of all ages use attention-seeking ploys, and in older children there are often changes in the application and quality of their school work. Rapid mood swings often prevail. One minute the child is highly excitable, whilst the next finds him or her sullen and withdrawn. Some children display disrespect to adults, rules and regulations. Other children become very aggressive, violent and destructive. Children of all ages can go through a spell of clinging to either or both parents and seeming fearful of letting them out of their sight.

All these manifestations of unsociable or unusual behaviour are products of unidentified disturbed feelings. The child does not understand what is happening to each of the parents, and neither does the child understand what is happening to him- or herself. Some of the child's feelings are generated by the atmosphere, tensions and unhappiness within the household, whilst others are engendered by a fertile imagination. They are all signals which tell us that the child is uncomfortable, and his or her abnormal behaviour must be seen as symptoms needing careful exploration and management.

Men and women in conflict naturally feel everburdened by their own worries, anxieties and fears. When emotions run high, it is difficult rapidly to change demeanour when confronted by a friend rather than a foe! A partner who is charged with anger or overwhelmed by injustice finds it hard to switch to being the loving, tolerant and patient parent. If the child is displaying unacceptable behaviour, then tolerance and patience are in short supply. When the parent lets off steam, the result tends to be further bad feelings in the form of recrimination and remorse. Desperation and a sense of failure quickly descend, and the spiral winds even further down.

One area which causes much pain to the child is divided loyalties. Parents need to be vigilant with regard to preserving the right of the child to have two parental relationships which are healthy and whole. Both mother and father have an important part in the child's life, and restraint is required whenever a parent is tempted to 'spill the beans' or 'put the child in the picture'. Attempting to colour the child's image of mother or father does untold damage to *both* relationships. Similarly, it is totally unfair to ask a child to take sides. He or she is put in an impossible position, for to choose one parent means the child is forced to deny his or her love for the other, and this can seem like betrayal to the child.

A great fear of the child is that he or she is to blame for the conflict or discord. The child needs constant reassurance that he or she has neither caused nor exacerbated the situation. He or she may also be confused about the nature of love. If this is the child's first exposure to poor relationships, then he or she may fear that *all* relationships end this way. Another problem to the child is in understanding that it is possible to continue loving one family member whilst withdrawing love from another. He or she sometimes mistakenly believes that there are two states, namely loving and hating, and when you love everyone is included, and when you hate you can't possibly love anyone. This is based very much on the child's own temporary mood swings. When he or she is in a bad mood everything goes wrong, and when he or she is in a good mood everything is all right with the world. The child needs extra reassurance to dispel the fear that mother or father may begin to hate or be indifferent towards him or her as a matter of course.

In the context of a child's short life, a few weeks is a very long time. When discord drags on from months to years, the child frequently begins to believe that discomfort and misery are his or her lot. When living with conflict becomes the normal pattern of living, the child learns to respond to each moment. Sometimes he or she is very fearful, and at other times he or she is relieved but worried as to what will happen next. The child slowly begins to build his or her own kind of barriers to shut out the hurt and the anxiety. In the short term this protects, but in the longer term it jeopardises the child's own personal relationships and his or her ability to allow people to get close.

Children, like adults, are unique beings, and each child is affected by conflict and discomfort in his or her own particular way. Parents considering staying together for the sake of the child or children need to take into account the adaptability of each child, their ability to maintain a healthy and loving relationship with each child, and the co-operation and determination of their partner to do likewise. Relatives and friends may also contribute to the emotional security of the child by just being there and being unchanged. A daily timetable and framework of home life with little alteration, alongside a continuing standard of discipline and codes of conduct, will also give the child a sense of stability and an anchor. If this is supported by the explicit love of both parents, the child will accept and adapt without too much pain.

THE EFFECT OF THE SPLIT UPON THE CHILDREN

The period immediately before the split occurs is usually the most distressing time for both parents and children. The peak of the whole process of heart searching and decision-making reaches a crescendo at the time of parting. Before this there is often an atmosphere of suspicion, antagonism, hostility and blame. Sometimes there is whispering or bickering, whilst at other times there is angry silence or expressions of sadness and remorse. These and other strong feelings give the child a very sinister flavour of what is going on. He or she feels afraid and insecure because of his or her ignorance. The fear of the unknown is the greatest fear of all. The child needs to know what is happening so that he or she can chase away the fantasies that lurk in his or her mind. The child also needs to know of the options open to his or her parents and how each might affect him or her. He or she may want to state his or her own wants, needs, expectations and fears, and wise parents will listen to the child with respect. The child needs honest answers to his or her questions, and each parent will need carefully to sift through all that has gone on, so that the child is given facts which are uncluttered by the interpretations of the parent.

Children from about the age of three onwards will ask the same questions again and again. This is not to harass adults but stems from a genuine need to be persuaded that what is happening *is* happening. The reactions of the child arise from grief, and just as the newly bereaved need to go over the circumstances of the death repeatedly in order to internalise the facts, so the child needs to turn all the details over repeatedly in his or her own mind in order to believe what is happening with both head and heart. Parents need to answer the questions as often as requested, so that there is no doubt that a clear picture develops in the child's mind.

Parents need to prepare and discuss their combined communications to the child about the split. As changes take place and their many decisions take shape, the parents must thrash out their whole approach to giving the information to the child. Where there is more than one child, then the parents need to consider each child and alter their approach accordingly. The crux of the matter is that the trust of a child is a very delicate ingredient, and once a parent has lost or tarnished that trust, it is hard to regain it.

Before the split, the child has one home and two parents. If the child is assured that, no matter what happens, he or she will still have all three, even though one parent may live at another address, the child will feel he or she has something secure and abiding. This must surely be the principal aim of the parents at this extremely emotional and often stormy time.

When the split occurs, the child is often in a state of shock. There is always a sense of panic and disbelief, even though the event may have been talked through many times beforehand. Some children try to deny there is any change, and pretend that everything is as it used to be. This adds an extra pressure upon the parent who is regularly caring for the child, at a time when the parent is impeded by his or her own reactions to the change, and feels like burying his or her own head in the sand too. The parent finds it difficult to determine which feelings belong to the child and which are his or her own. In order to clarify this, the parent needs to encourage the child to express how he or she feels, so that assumptions can be checked out and followed through.

Older and more articulate children are able to voice their thoughts and their feelings, but they sometimes need an adult to give them permission to do so. They are sometimes very anxious about protecting their parents from being overburdened, and so they hide their unresolved feelings. Mothers or fathers who can enable their older child to trust them with their feelings find that this strengthens rather than weakens their relationship, and often leads to a sharing of coping strategies. Younger children need help as they try to put their feelings into words. This can be done by stories and drawings. Tears are a therapy and bring great relief to children of all ages. It is important to encourage the child to shed enough tears and not to feel ashamed by them.

For most children, the impact of the split is a new experience. They may have imagined how it would feel and take effect, but underlying these fantasies there will have been the vain hope that a magical reconciliation would take place. When the split does happen, the next chain of new experiences begins to emerge. These may include removal to another home; a change of school, friends and social life; a lower standard of living; loss of contact with one set of grandparents and other relatives; loss of a regular and available model on which to base male or female images, and many other such changes dependent upon circumstances.

These changes, however, are a great source of challenge, which most children welcome. Few see them as threatening, and rising to meet and adapt to these new experiences helps children to accept and find new ways of investing themselves in their new life.

Relatives, friends, neighbours and teachers need to know fairly quickly that the split has occurred. This will help the child to be open and will dispel the sinister implications of secrecy. It will also enable other adults to interpret any odd behaviour and make necessary allowance for it. They may also be helpful in identifying other one-parent families in the vicinity, and thus help the child to accept that he or she does not stick out like a sore thumb, but is part of a very common phenomenon in our society. Recent statistics tell us that one in five children will have divorced parents by the time they reach the age of 16. Therefore it is reasonable to accept that 20 per cent of each class in school are children with divorced parents. The children of unmarried parents are not included in this figure, so the chances that some of your child's friends are also of broken relationships are very great indeed.

Children do suffer when their parents separate, but provided they have sensitive parents who don't make rash promises and who consider carefully the way the split occurs and the way feelings are handled, they can accept and adapt very successfully. The key is in involving the child to his or her capacity depending upon his or her age and character. It is essential to remember that there are many losses involved for the child, and he or she needs to grieve for them. This is a natural process, and provided the child is encouraged to express his or her feelings and get them out into the open, he or she will gradually work through the stages of shock, panic, disbelief, anger, despair, frustration, searching, regression, and guilt to the resolution of the grief by acceptance and adaptation. In all this the child needs to be assured of the unchanging love of both parents, if at all possible, as rejection is probably the worst feeling of all.

DECISIONS ABOUT CUSTODY AND ACCESS

When parents part, there are many critical questions surrounding the maintenance, quality of life and general well-being of the child or children. Who is going to accept the day-to-day caring of each child? Where will they live? Is it possible for there to be little disruption? What kind of financial arrangements are required? How is the relationship with the leaving parent going to be maintained? Who is going to organise this? Who will make the policy decisions about the future for each child? Are the parents able reasonably to negotiate and work out what is best for their child or children in the light of their individual circumstances? What happens if either parent takes a new partner? All these issues need exploration, clarification and a child-centred approach, in that the needs of the child must take priority over any personal considerations.

Where couples are divorcing, there is a legal requirement in that the judge has to examine the arrangements for the children, and rarely is a decree absolute granted until this part of the procedure is complete. Both parents are informed by the court of the date when the judge will see them, and this meeting is informal in that it is held in a private room at the court with only the judge, court clerk, court welfare officer, the parents, and their legal advisers if they so wish, present. The parents need to have a prepared statement of the arrangements with them.

During the meeting the judge will have to decide whether the arrangements are 'satisfactory', 'the best that can be devised in the circumstances', or 'impracticable for the party or parties appearing before the court to make any such arrangements'. If it is not possible to arrive at any of these three, then there will be a delay in the granting of a decree absolute. The judge may advise the parents to seek help in making their decisions. In most large cities there are now excellent conciliation services which provide safe facilities where the couple can focus on making decisions about the child or children. The carefully selected and specially trained conciliator helps to reduce the personal and emotional input so that purposeful negotiating can take place. Recent surveys have confirmed that those couples who have availed themselves of the conciliation service sort out their arrangements with less spite, rancour and bitterness. In those areas where this service is as yet unavailable, the court welfare officer or a probation officer may undertake this role. The child in the middle needs to know that these important decisions are being made, and often it is the climate surrounding these decisions which make him or her either a beneficiary or a victim.

The question of the day-to-day management and care of each child may be governed by circumstances. For instance, if the father is leaving to start a new partnership, then it may not be convenient for the child or children to go with him. Some mothers feel that it is their prerogative to take on the 'care and control'. Many fathers feel this is unfair, and more are now putting forward their considered proposals stating their desire and capability as the continuing resident parent. Care and control is usually given to one parent, and the court tends to value the length of time a child has been with one parent or the other. The last thing the court wants is disruption for the child. The whereabouts of other children of the family is also taken into account, as it is believed that the family needs to be held together if it is at all possible. If the children are staying in the marital home, then they will be able to continue at the same school, have the same friends and follow their normal social pattern. When this is not possible, the child requires a great deal of emotional support in order to cope with the upheaval.

'Custody' can be given to either the daily parent or the order can be given to both parents jointly. Joint custody means that both parents have to discuss and negotiate policy decisions regarding their child or children. These will be issues such as education, medical care matters, the moral and/or religious upbringing of the child, and marriage. This involvement reassures everyone that the child still has two parents. The divorce is totally between the parents and there is no divorce between parent and child or children.

Parents living away from their child have the right to see

that child regularly, unless it can be proved in court that such access would be detrimental to the child. The access order can be for frequent visits, overnight stays or a combination of both. Usually the court makes out an order for 'reasonable access' and the parents are then left to sort out the most convenient arrangement. If there is a dispute, however, the order can be very precise in detailing the frequency, the time and the place. The future arrangements as the child grows up and circumstances change may be done through the court, but many parents find it much easier if they can negotiate out of court and between themselves as and when the need arises.

Parents who are not married find they, too, have definite negotiations to work through with regard to the short- and long-term caring of their child or children. The only way a mother can secure financial support from the father for their child is by taking affiliation proceedings in the magistrates' court. It is also possible for a parent to apply for an order of access in the High Court, county court or the magistrates' court. The attitude of society towards unmarried parents has changed significantly in recent years, and if the parent has lived in the same home as the child the court may well agree that access would be the best decision for the child. Whilst most unmarried mothers insist on having both care and control and custody of the child, there are an increasing number of unmarried fathers who want to be the full-time parent to the child. There are facilities for unmarried fathers also to apply for the right to have the child living with them and for custody, but the onus is on them to prove that the mother is unfit or unwilling to care for the child. Other circumstances may be because of her death or because the child has been taken into care.

Care and control, custody and access matters require unemotional and precise attention to detail. A skilled lawyer is recommended. It is hard to work out practical arrangements when intense feelings abound and most parents feel very emotional about their children. The help of specialised people such as court welfare officers, probation officers, conciliation counsellors, marriage counsellors, Citizen's Advice Bureau workers and empathetic listeners at the Samaritans can be very positive. It is also necessary to remember that the court orders are not for ever and either parent can reapply to the court for variance at any time.

Living with the court orders may prove to be very different to the expectations when they were made. In the time before the split the child saw both parents for different periods of the day. The parent supervising usually gave praise and meted out punishment as appropriate. The everyday decisions may have been shared, depending on who was 'on duty' at the time. Once one parent leaves the home, the remaining parent suddenly has 24-hour responsibility. He or she is never 'off duty', but is always 'on call'. This is a big responsibility, and added to the stress of other spin-offs from the split it can seem overwhelming.

The support of other parents in similar situations cannot be quantified, and it is good to know that others are having similar difficulties; that they are coping and that you can share coping strategies. Adjusting to being a single parent is not easy, but the relief from constant rowing or hostility may go some way to compensate. Some men and women, however, have become so entrenched in attack and defence, that they find it hard to work from a position of assertion rather than submission or aggression. It is important to determine the pattern of your own responses and to discard any that are habits and now inappropriate since the adversary has gone!

Access can cause problems, and these need to be reduced to a minimum. The child may be very distressed when leaving the daily parent, and equally upset when he or she has to return and leave the absent parent. This is under-standable initially, and the child needs lots of reassurance that he or she still has two parents and has not 'lost' one. Once the child has successfully visited and returned home several times, he or she will absorb it into the normal pattern of living and no longer find it disturbing. It does require the patience, understanding and perseverance of both parents.

The absent parent often finds it very hard to develop a natural relationship with the child. One of the biggest problems is the short amount of time available. Trust is an essential part of relationship-building, and the child may be very suspicious of adults initially. From the child's viewpoint the two important people in his or her life have made big changes which have probably caused him or her some heartache.

The short visit often means that mum or dad becomes the Saturday Outing parent who offers pleasurable activities and little discipline. He or she is in danger of becoming the indulgent 'uncle' or 'aunt' figure, and after a short time both child and parent find this frustrating and artificial. The child sometimes seizes the opportunity to play one parent against the other, and this must be discouraged, as should the temptation to persuade the child to become spy or go-between.

Decisions about custody and access must be seen by both parents as an entirely separate part of their splitting which needs a different focus when considering the outcome. Instead of working towards taking out their investment in their relationship, they now have to work at increasing and developing in new ways their relationship with the child. The focus must be on continuing and building their investment in the child/parent relationship. The best interests of the child are the primary consideration. Couples have the right and opportunity to split if the relationship doesn't work out, but the role of parent is forever! A bad parent is still a parent.

Co-operation, patience and understanding not only relieve the tension and animosity, but also provide the child with examples of good negotiation. Children use their parents as models and copy their responses and behaviour. Negotiations that are free of recrimination and vindictiveness provide the child with a model for negotiating his or her own sometimes difficult decisions.

The skilled and sensitive helpers in the community offer specialist help, and those couples who receive this assistant openly acknowledge the short- and long-term benefits this has on the child. They also often find that a lot of the heat is diffused and other negotiations follow with much less struggle.

THE FUTURE AND NEW RELATIONSHIPS

The first few weeks after the split are often a time of rapid change. The child is required to adapt to many alterations in his or her lifestyle. The first and perhaps the most difficult adjustment is in getting used to one parent living away from home. The child will need to go through the very natural process of grief, for he or she has lost the daily contact with that parent. If the child can express his or her pain openly without being embarrassed, ashamed or guilty, and verbalise his or her fears about the future, then he or she will arrive at acceptance and adaptation much faster.

The daily parent becomes a very important figure during the first few weeks, and it is often necessary to give many assurances to allay the fear that this parent is also going to walk out. If the absent parent has abandoned his or her responsibilities towards the child, then these assurances are critical. Some children resist sleep, play truant from school or fake illness in order to 'watch' or 'keep' the daily parent within the home.

Grief in children often manifests itself in difficult or regressive behaviour. The child wants to draw attention to him- or herself so that he or she will not be forgotten, and it is the child's fear of being abandoned which is the hardest to bear. Soiling and bedwetting, biting and disturbed eating and sleeping patterns are all signals displaying a general dis-ease. These are usually only temporary and gradually disappear. Children who suffer in this way for more than a week or two do need special help, and the doctor is the first resort.

Well-meaning relatives and friends often overburden the eldest child following separation or divorce. If the father leaves the household, the oldest boy is now exhorted to be 'the man of the house'. If it is the mother who has left, then the oldest girl is urged to be 'the little mother'. This is a terrible burden to place on young shoulders, especially when the child is wanting comfort and help. Children can take on extra responsibilities and often enjoy this, but the daily parent and each individual child need to negotiate what is appropriate and how the chores of the household can be shared so that no one feels overworked. Each child can gain by enjoying the satisfaction of sharing in the tasks, which is far better than feeling a big sense of failure due to the unrealistic expectations of others.

The job of maintaining a pattern of life for the children which has as little change as possible is seldom easy for the daily parent. Children need to be involved in the discussions and implementation of change if at all possible. Once they know the reasons why, most children accept and adapt. Rebellion and stubborness are the result of assumptions and misunderstanding in most cases. Spelling out the information is time-consuming, but it cuts a lot of corners in the long run.

Home is very important to a child. It is his or her fortress, citadel, territory. If the split necessitates a move, then the child needs to know as soon as possible. One way of explaining the need to move might be that instead of having one old home the child is now going to have two new ones; one where he or she will live most of the time and another where he or she will be able to visit and stay with the absent parent. The attitude of the daily parent is important. If he or she can see the move as a new beginning, rather than as a poor substitute for what he or she has become accustomed to, his or her enthusiasm will show. The parent is on the way to a different way of life, and can choose whether to see this as a threat or a challenge. The parent's choice will rub off on the child, and this must influence the parent's general attitude.

A change of schools is sometimes necessary at this point, and again the child needs to know *why* this is necessary. Many children in our mobile society move to new schools and quickly adapt to their new environment. The best way is to take it a day at a time and recognise that there will be some grief for the friends and teachers the child has left behind. If contacts can be arranged with old friends, this is often very valuable and helps the child to accept that there is some continuity in his or her life. The child very quickly takes out his or her investments in the old school and his or her relationships there, and begins to reinvest in the new school and feel part of it.

One area that seems to cause many problems is the

avoidance of contact with grandparents and relatives of the absent parent. This can be very distressing to the child, and he or she may feel feelings have to be hidden because the daily parent might judge the child to be disloyal or partisan. Ongoing relationships, with grandparents in particular, are advisable. The child needs as much love and support as he or she can get to help him or her through this difficult time, and to be cut off from people who have been used to giving out such love just adds to the child's discomfort. Decisions about relationships with relatives need to be given the same kind of approach as the question of access. The grandparents, aunts, uncles and cousins will hold those titles forever, and it is important for the child to understand that he or she still belongs to this extended family. If the child's needs are put first, then each parent will feel they are achieving good parenting despite any sense of failure they feel with regard to the breakdown of their partner relationship.

If yours has been the kind of family which welcomes friends to the home and makes return visits, the decision as to whether to continue as before may be hard to make. Children usually love visitors and visiting, and if this can be maintained, even if only initially, it will add to the sense of security and continuity experienced by your child. The split is a new beginning, and each partner has fresh opportunities to make new friends and relationships. Single parent groups such as Gingerbread organise activities for both parent and child. They include outings and economic holidays. This not only brings enjoyment but also the chance to meet other parents and children in similar situations. In such a group the child will have the opportunity to see how other children cope successfully, and also he or she will begin to feel part of a larger group within the community and therefore more normal.

When new close relationships are formed, it is advisable to introduce the child as early as possible. This requires care and explanations, with an emphasis on the fact that this is a new person with a very different role. Sometimes resentments build up if the child misunderstands and believes the special friend is attempting to replace mum or dad. The child usually prefers to meet the new person formally at first, and needs time gradually to test out and begin to build trust in the relationship. This seems reasonable when one recognises that he or she has recently learned that adults hurt! A child needs time to get over initial reactions before contemplating any long-term plans, and so the child needs to be considered when pacing the development of a new relationship. The older child will appreciate being involved as the parent makes his or her decisions. The child needs to feel he or she is a very real part of the parent's life, and sometimes it is easy to forget to be explicit about this.

If a parent does take a new partner, then it is important to make it known to the child that the new partner and his or her children are not replacing the child in the parent's life. Children often see love and affection as being like a cake which is cut into several pieces. They sometimes think that by the time the plate is handed round to them, there are only crumbs left. The child needs much reassurance and help in accepting that each love in the parent's life is different and important. He or she needs to be very sure that the parent wants him or her and needs him or her because the child wants and needs the parent so much.

If parenting is done well, children of separated or divorced couples are well adjusted and will have learned very early on in life about conflict and pain. They will have also learned to accept and adapt to new circumstances and situations. The lasting benefit is the knowledge that they are versatile and flexible and most of all copers. They may have come through a hard school, but their experiences will have made them more understanding and tolerant of human behaviour. Many children of separated and divorced parents lead happy, successful and contented lives because they know their parents love them whatever happens. This gives them an inner security which cannot be underestimated. If they have picked up the art of honest negotiation and conflict management during the process of their parents' parting, then they will have excellent techniques for skilfully handling their own personal relationships in the future.

Glossary of legal terms

Access A right granted by a court allowing the parent not granted custody and/or the grandparent specific or indefinite time with the child. 'Reasonable access' leaves the parents free to make their own arrangements for access. 'Defined access' is what the court determines. Those arrangements should be when the parents cannot agree.

Acknowledgement of service Form accompanying the petition sent by the court to the respondent. The form poses questions about the respondent's intentions and wishes in reponse to the petition. When the form is returned to the court, the service of petition is established.

Affidavit A statement in writing and on oath of facts known personally to the maker of the statement for use by the court without the maker being present in court. Documents referred to in the statement may be annexed to the statement and are then said to be exhibited.

Affiliation An order of the court obliging the father of a child born out of wedlock to maintain it.

Answer The reply to a divorce petition or cross-petition refuting the allegations in the petition or cross-petition.

Application A document stating the order sought from the court. All divorce proceedings are begun by filing a notice of application. The divorce court offices have standard forms available.

Beneficial interest The right of a person to use or occupy a property and to have a share in the proceeds if it is sold, even if he or she has no legal ownership.

Calderbank letter Letter written by the husband's solicitor offering a lump sum settlement out of court in response to a notice that a court hearing is being sought for hearing an application for maintenance. If the wife refuses the offer and at a court hearing she is awarded less than the offer, she may risk having to pay the husband's costs incurred after the date of the offer.

Care and control The responsibility for everyday care and management of the child, and the decisions involved.

In chambers Consideration by a judge or registrar in private of an application which by the rules of the court does not require to be considered in open court.

Child of the family A child of both parties to the marriage or any other child (not being a foster child) whom the parties have treated as a child of their family.

Clean break The principle applied by the divorce court when dissolving marriage of very short duration or of very young couples, of limiting liability of the one spouse for the other's maintenance to the shortest possible period after divorce.

Common fund A more generous basis for assessing the costs of a successful litigant, enabling him or her to reclaim expenses reasonably incurred by him or her in preparing his or her case and not just his or her solicitor/client costs.

Conciliation A way of patiently and genuinely working towards agreement by both parties on issues concerning the children (custody and access), finance and the division of the property and possessions. Conciliators working with the Conciliation Service, domestic court welfare officers and probation officers offer informal, confidential help, provided both parties are willing to participate.

Constructive desertion When a spouse leaves the matrimonial home with just cause.

Co-respondent A person with whom the respondent is alleged to have committed adultery.

Counsel A barrister.

Cross-petition When the respondent seeks a divorce by putting forward reasons for the breakdown of the marriage which differ from those stated by the petitioner.

Custody The right to make major decisions concerning the

child, up until the child reaches 18. Major decisions include upbringing, education, change of religion, consent to marry, etc. This right can be given to one or both parents.

Decree absolute The order dissolving the marriage.

Decree nisi The provisional dissolution of a marriage which will not be made absolute (final) for six weeks, and then only if arrangements for care of any children of the family are satisfactory in the court's view.

Divorce court The High Court or any county court specially designated by the Lord Chancellor for hearing undefended divorce petitions.

Domicile The permanent home of a person or the place where the law presumes or the court finds that he or she intends permanently to reside.

Equity (of a house) The right of a mortgagor (borrower) to deal with the property as owner, subject only to the repayment of the mortgage (loan) to the mortgagee (lender).

Family assets Property acquired by husband and wife, or singly, with the intention of use by the family as a whole during their joint lives.

Filing Term used when giving petition, affidavits and notices of application to the court officer for sealing and serving.

Green form Name given to a scheme whereby a limited amount of legal advice and assistance is given either free or for a reduced assessed contribution.

Injunction An order of the High Court or a county court requiring a person to do or to refrain from doing a particular act, on pain of being punished if he or she does not obey. The commonest punishment for disobedience is imprisonment.

Jurisdiction The power or authority of a court or judge to grant relief, including the territorial and temporal limits within which the court or judge may exercise that power or authority.

Jurisprudence The knowledge of laws, customs and rights of men and women necessary for the due administration of justice.

Legal aid Advice and/or representation by a lawyer (solicitor or barrister) at no charge, or less than full charge, to the litigant. The scheme, which is Government funded, is administered by the Law Society. The grant of legal aid is dependent on the merits of the case and on the litigant's means (both capital and income). The grant covers the cost of the litigant's case; it does not cover the litigant for the costs of his or her opponent's case supposing he or she is unfortunate enough to be ordered to bear the opponent's costs. Any costs that the litigant recovers from the opponent will be chargeable with the cost that the legal aid fund has incurred in providing the litigant with legal advice and/or representation.

Liable relative proceedings Proceedings taken when the legally responsible person fails to maintain husband or wife and/or child.

Nominal order An order for a nominal sum (e.g. 5 pence per year) of maintenance which can be reviewed or varied if circumstances change. Usually set up when payment cannot be made (e.g the legally responsible person is unemployed and without adequate means) or is not at that time needed.

Notice of application The first formal approach to the court setting out all the details of the application and beginning with the words 'Take notice that . . .'.

Nullity of marriage A decree declaring that a supposed marriage is null and void.

Petitioner The person who makes the first move in beginning divorce proceedings by filing the petition.

Postal divorce Common name for an undefended divorce where the facts submitted by the petitioner and verified on affidavit are considered by the registrar at the divorce court without either party or their representing solicitors being present. Once the registrar is satisfied that the grounds for divorce are proved, he or she issues a certificate to that effect and arranges a date for the formal decree nisi to be pronounced by a judge. Both parties receive a copy of the decree from the court by post.

Prayer The formal request by the petitioner or respondent for court orders listed in the petition or answer (e.g. costs, custody, etc.).

Putative father The supposed or reputed father of a child born out of wedlock.

Registrar A lawyer appointed by the Lord Chancellor to take responsibility for dealing with most of the applications for divorce.

Reply A Formal response and/or defence filed by the petitioner in answer to the reply and/or cross-petition of the respondent.

Respondent The spouse who is not the petitioner.

Sealing by the court The official court stamp used on all formal documents filed at the court office and on all orders and decress issued by the court.

Service A term used to describe the way in which the parties concerned receive the petition, notices of application, orders and decrees. Some need to be served personally, others are served by post; some are served by the court and some by the person issuing them or by their representative.

Special procedure See postal divorce.

Summons A court command for the appearance at a court hearing of a person against whom a claim or complaint has been made.

Testamentary guardian Someone appointed by will or deed to be guardian to a minor.

Ward of court A minor given the protection of the court which then assumes responsibility for all major decisions relating to the well-being of the child.

Sources of help in the community

Access Centres

These facilities are safe and warm premises where parents can take their child or children for the time of their access visit. The facility is provided usually by the co-operation of both statutory and voluntary caring people. The centres are nomally open on Saturdays between 9 am and 5 pm and play areas, games, toys and refreshments are available.

Many parents are presented with difficulties in regard to regular access visits. The access centre is free and gives parents the opportunity to spend time with their child in a pleasant and stimulating environment. The resident parent is reassured, particularly when he or she is unable to welcome the access visit in his or her home. More access centres are being opened. Ask at CAB or the local library.

Association of British Introduction Agencies (ABIA)

Dating agencies and marriage bureaux aim to introduce men to women and vice versa for the purpose of marriage and/or friendship. They do this by personal introduction after computer comparison or the list method (forwarding a list of all, or selected, clients on joining, and updating the list regularly).

The services vary, as do the costs (£20-£100). Membership is from the age of 18 years upwards, whilst the upper age limit ranges from 55 to 80 years.

The standards of agencies have been questioned and the ABIA now has members which adhere to a code of practice. It is important to check that membership is currently maintained, as only complaints about members can be processed by ABIA. A list of current members can be obtained free of charge from ABIA, 29 Manchester Street, LONDON W1.

Association of Separated and Divorced Catholics

Information about this voluntary organisation can be obtained from the local Roman Catholic church.

British Association of Counsellors (BAC)

There are many private counselling practitioners offering confidential help and support to men and women with relationship and family problems. The therapy is usually feelings-centred, and appointments last for about an hour and can be for one or both partners. Regular further sessions at approximately weekly intervals are often arranged.

Fees vary according to geographical location. The average charge is £20 per session in the provinces and more in the cities.

BAC membership involves experience, training and the following of the Association's definition of counselling and code of ethics and practice.

A list of accredited counsellors and trainers (who often run workshops on developing assertiveness, confidence-building and self-development, etc.) is prepared by BAC. The address is BAC, 37 Sheep Street, RUGBY, Warwickshire. Telephone: 0788 78328/9.

Catholic Marriage Advisory Service (CMAC)

This service trains men and women volunteers of the Roman Catholic Church to help anyone with marriage or family problems. Courses for engaged couples are also offered by branches in most areas. Details from priests or from CMAC, 15 Lansdowne Road, LONDON W11 3AJ. Telephone: 01-727 0141.

Child Poverty Action Group (CPAG)

This voluntary organisation aims to campaign for changes in policy in order to stamp out poverty, and to fight for a fairer future for children. They offer help and training in welfare rights and benefits. The Citizens' Rights Office offers free information, advice and an advocacy service to poor familes. Further details from CPAG, 1–5 Bath Street, LONDON EC1V 9PY.

Citizens' Advice Bureau (CAB)

Both paid and voluntary workers have been carefully selected and trained to give advice and information to anyone seeking help. Their bank of knowledge is regularly updated and is second to none. The service is free and confidential. Many Bureaux have additional services which include debt counselling, legal help from a practising solicitor, financial guidance by an accountant, and experts in the calculation of welfare rights and benefits. Selected CABs also have tribunal units attached.

Department of Social Security (DSS)

Most state benefits are administered by the DSS. A freefone service is available in all areas of the country giving general advice and guidance on social security benefits. A postal service distributes relevant leaflets and claim forms. Information regarding cash help, help for one-parent families, retirement pensions, National Insurance contributions rates, benefit rates and the like is available.

It is acceptable to ask for a confidential interview, although it may mean waiting for a little extra time. More details can be obtained by telephoning 100 and asking the operator for freefone DSS.

Divorce Court Welfare Officer

The Court Welfare Service is provided by the probation service. The court welfare officer is a probation officer who has received special training and extra experience in family relationships. If the judge is not satisfied with the arrangements for the children when the case is heard, he or she will adjourn the court and ask for more information to be prepared. This information is frequently collated by the court welfare officer, who will discuss the issues with both parents and, if appropriate, the children. The prepared report will then go to the judge, with copies provided for each parent to see and to comment upon if they so wish.

In areas where there is no conciliation service, the court welfare officer is frequently called upon by the judge to act as conciliator.

Divorce Registry

The principal divorce court for the London area. Forms for the petition and for the statements of arrangements for the children are available from divorce courts and the Divorce Registry. A free booklet, *Undefended Divorce – a Guide for the Petitioner Acting without a Solicitor*, is also available. The address is Divorce Registry, Somerset House, Strand, LONDON WC2R 1LF. The divorce county courts can be found under 'court' or 'county courts' in the telephone directory.

Families Need Fathers (FNF)

This organisation is a voluntary self-help group of parents, primarily concerned with the problems of maintaining a child's relationship with both parents during and following separation and divorce. The group produces leaflets and helpful information. Men and women with access and custody difficulties are offered immediate support, help and advice. The organisation promotes equal parental rights, with the well-being of the child as the principal aim. Addresses are: FNF, 27 Old Gloucester Street, LONDON WC1N 3XX; and Scottish FNF, 7B Octavia Street, KIRKCALDY, Fife KY2 5HH.

Gingerbread

This registered charity is the association for lone parents and their children. Local groups throughout Great Britain offer self-help, social outlets, support, children's and family activities. Gingerbread also arranges economic holidays and outings. Organisation of the groups varies from place to place, but many are a lifeline and a source of stimulation and encouragement when they are needed most. For local information ask at the public library or at CAB. The head office address is Gingerbread, 35 Wellington Street, LONDON WC2E 7BN. Telephone: 01-248 6840.

Jewish Marriage Council

Another agency comparable to Relate and CMAC for members of the Jewish faith. Details from the Jewish Marriage Council, 23 Ravenshurst Avenue, LONDON NW4 4EL. Telephone: 01-203 6311.

Joint Council for the Welfare of Immigrants (JCWI)

This is an independent voluntary organisation specialising in immigration and nationality law and practice. They answer telephone calls from any part of the country, and advise on any aspect of immigration and nationality. The address is JCW1, 115 Old Street, LONDON EC1V 9JP. Telephone: 01-251 8706.

Law Centre Federation

Local law centres have full-time staff and can handle a case from beginning to end, including representation at court. The service is generally free, but restricted to clients who cannot afford to pay legal fees. The service varies across the country, so there is a need to make initial enquiries. A stamped addressed envelope will ensure a list of law centres and information about the work. The Legal Action Group publishes a directory of legal advice and law centres, and the local CAB and public library should have copies. The address is Law Centre Federation, Duchess House, Warren Street, LONDON NW1.

Mothers Apart from Their Children (MATCH)

A support group for women living apart from their children as a result of separation or divorce. Groups exist in London, Birmingham and Bristol, and women in other parts of the country are put in touch with others in similar circumstances. By correspondence, they provide each other with help, support and understanding. Further details from MATCH, c/o BM Problems, LONDON WC1N 3XX.

National Council for the Divorced and Separated (NCDS)

Branches flourish throughout the UK. The aim of the Council is 'to identify and promote the interests and welfare of all persons whose marriages have ended in divorce or separation, and to provide a channel for the formation and representation of opinion on all matters of concern to such persons'.

Branches provide a regular social get-together, outings and holidays. A welfare officer is appointed in each branch, and counselling, advice and information are available. A national welfare consultant cares for individual members who are not attached to branches. Documentary proof of divorce or separation is required before membership is approved. More details from NCDS, 13 High Street, Little Shelford, CAMBRIDGE CB2 5ES.

National Council for One-Parent Families

This charitable organisation attempts to secure financial, legal and social equality for lone parents and their children. Their concerns cover poverty, employment, housing, legal problems and stress. The information service is well used, and up-to-date leaflets and information sheets for parents are available. The advice department offers help, advice and counselling, mainly by telephone and by letter. One-Parent Families' advisers also represent lone parents at appeal tribunals. This organisation is especially useful to unmarried ex-partners bringing up children alone. For further details please write to the National Council for One-Parent Families, 255 Kentish Town Road, LONDON NW5 2LX. The advice service operates from 9.15 am until 5.15 pm each weekday except Wednesday.

National Council for Voluntary Organisations (NCVO)

This service offers addresses of local councils for voluntary service and voluntary service organisations throughout the country. The local service has a membership of most of the self-help and caring groups, alongside other voluntary groups. It is a useful source of addresses and information regarding help, and also for linking men and women to worthwhile voluntary work once they feel able to offer help to others. Working with other volunteers in one of many varied activities or projects is a great help when trying to set up new social networks, and for promoting confidence and a sense of being needed. The address is NCVO, 26 Bedford Square, LONDON WC1B 3HU.

National Family Conciliation Council (NFCC)

Family conciliation can offer help by means of selected and trained counsellors when a couple who are splitting cannot agree over important issues such as those concerning the family. The aim of this charitable organisation is to help and encourage parents to make rational and reasonable decisions together in the best interests of everyone, but most importantly the children. Local family conciliation services provide an excellent service, in that men and women are given time, space and opportunity to negotiate and make joint decisions on custody, access and related matters. Couples with disputes over property or money can also use this service. Details of local facilities can be found in the telephone directory or CAB. The address of the national office is NFCC, 34 Milton Road, SWINDON, Wiltshire SN1 5JA. Telephone: 0793 618486.

National Federation of Solo Clubs (NFSC)

There are Solo Clubs in most of the cities and large towns, and the chief aim is to provide friendship for widowed, divorced, separated and single people under the age of 65. Holidays and outings (which can also include children) are organised, and a newsletter is published monthly. The meetings are usually weekly, and a host or hostess welcomes shy and new members. Each branch has a welfare officer to visit sick members and to help with problems. The head office in Birmingham also houses an advice centre. More details from NFSC, Rooms 7/8 Ruskin Chambers, 191 Corporation Street, BIRMINGHAM B4 6RY. Telephone: 021-236 2879.

Nexus

This is a world-wide organisation for unattached men and women. It offers opportunity to join social groups, make telephone friends and find new partners. A monthly bulletin is sent to members. The first-year subscription is £65, but reduces considerably in the second and subsequent years. The address is Nexus, Nexus House, Blackstock Road, LONDON, N4. Telephone: 01-359 7656/6703.

Probation Service

Skilled probation officers often offer conciliation facilities in areas where there is no family conciliation service. They also have skills in helping people with marriage, family and relationship problems. Addresses and telephone numbers of local offices can be found in the telephone directory under 'probation'.

Relate (National Marriage Guidance)

There are many branches throughout the UK working to standards supervised by the parent body. Counsellors are carefully selected and highly trained, with considerable in-service support. The service is confidential and person-centred. Couples are seen either together or separately, and often individuals seek help without their partner. Men and women with any kind of relationship or family problem are seen at any stage. Some seek help before setting up home together, during the union or before, during or after separation or divorce. Individual sessions last about an hour and can be repeated at approximately weekly intervals for as long as it takes. Some local branches offer places in small groups working on developing self-awareness, social skills and marriage/relationship enrichment. Sex therapy clinics are also attached to many local branches, where skilled therapists can be consulted. Local details can be found under 'marriage' in the telephone directory. More information and an excellent bookshop are at Relate, Herbert Gray College, Little Church Street, RUGBY, Warwickshire CV21 3AP. Telephone: 0788 73241.

Samaritans

Selected and trained volunteers supply a 24-hour telephone cover at every branch every day of the year. People of all ages and every circumstances ring them when they need someone. The service is used as a lifeline by the few who are suicidal, but the majority of callers are worried, perplexed, lonely and often needing to offload. The service is free and confidential. Befriending can ensue if the caller needs prolonged help and support. The telephone number of local branches is usually prominently displayed in all public places, and is always included in the Useful Numbers section at the front of the telephone directory.

Scottish Council for Single Parents

The Council offers help to all single parents, and gives individual help with practical and emotional problems. There is an information service and they produce leaflets and booklets. In some areas there are facilities for after-school and holiday care and a sitter service. Write to Scottish Council for Single Parents, 13 Gayfield Square, EDINBURGH EH1 3NX. Telephone: 031-556 3899.

Scottish Marriage Guidance Council (SMGC)

This organisation is run on very similar lines to Relate. The address is SMGC, 26 Frederick Street, EDINBURGH EH2 2JR. Telephone: 031-225 5006.

Shelter

This organisation is mainly concerned with housing and helping homeless people. The offices and Shelter-supported Housing Aid Centres throughout the UK offer advice and information on any housing query. Positive help is given to those looking for accommodation, and for those with rent-arrear problems there is help and support (advocacy in court in some areas). More details from Shelter, 88 Old Street, LONDON EC1V 9AX. Telephone: 01-253 0202.

Stepfamily – the National Stepfamily Association

This is a charitable organisation which aims to help those who are part of stepfamilies. The service offers support, advice and information with regard to family, legal, social and financial problems. Stepfamilies can take a variety of forms, including those which are stepfamilies only at week-ends or holidays. A quarterly newsletter and other relevant literature are available. Some areas have local groups, but there is a telephone line for those unable to join a group. The address of the head office is Stepfamily, 162 Tenison Road, CAMBRIDGE CB1 2DP. Telephone: 0223 460312 (general enquiries), 0223 460313 (counselling service).

Social Services departments

A duty officer is available for help without an appointment in an emergency. A social worker will help with family problems, and particularly any risk situation with children. A social worker can be a very positive support, both long term and in an emergency. The local offices are listed in the Useful Numbers section at the front of the telephone directory.